WILLIAM I

and

The Norman Conquest

by

FRANK BARLOW

THE ENGLISH UNIVERSITIES PRESS LTD

St. Paul's House   Warwick Lane   London E.C.4

DATE DUE

PRINTED AND BOUND IN ENGLAND FOR
THE ENGLISH UNIVERSITIES PRESS LTD, BY
HAZELL WATSON AND VINEY LTD AYLESBURY, BUCKS

Contents

Contents

This Book

gives a view of the conquest of England planned and carried out by Duke William of Normandy. No great historical revolution has been the work of one man alone; but few have been so individually inspired and directed as was this momentous enterprise. William's character and decisions determined the shattering effect which his small invasion in 1066 was to have on the kingdom. Moreover, William was a representative Norman. By studying his career we can begin to understand the way of life that he and his followers introduced into England, a culture which was to influence the country's development throughout the Middle Ages.

Many of the historical problems associated with the Conquest—especially the problem of what institutions the Normans destroyed and what they introduced—have been long, and are still, in debate. The author offers his own interpretation of the events and their effects.

Frank Barlow, M.A., D.Phil., is Professor of History in the University of Exeter. He is the author of *The Feudal Kingdom of England* and *The English Church, 1000–1066*, and the editor of *The Life of King Edward the Confessor*.

THE NORMAN DUCAL FAMILY

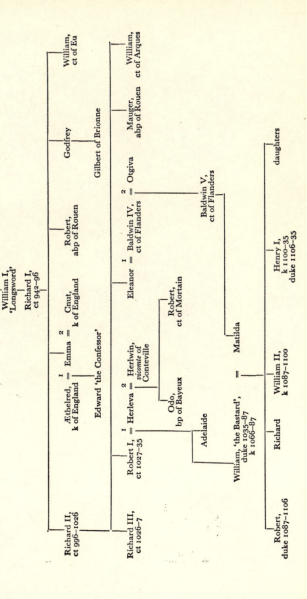

Acknowledgments

For some years I have taught 'The Norman Conquest of England' as a 'Special Subject' in History Finals and this book gives me the opportunity to present the opinions I have formed. I am grateful to my pupils for requiring me year after year to construe some of the basic texts because as a result I feel that I am beginning to understand them; and the monologue, to which a seminar is often reduced, although encouraging speculation and even extravagance, does have a purifying effect, for by repetition sillinesses become tiresome. Professor David Douglas's massive *William the Conqueror* appeared after I had written my first draft and offered me the chance, which I thankfully took, to check my detail against his and, when we differed in interpretation, to reconsider my views. I hope that I have profited by the opportunity. The general editor of the series gave me much good advice, which, I fear, I was not always skilful enough to follow. My colleagues, Mr G. W. Greenaway and Mr L. J. Lloyd, gave me comfort and help. Mrs Valerie A. Hawgood very kindly helped me to read the proofs.

Prologue

IN early Germanic society the most coveted reward was land. Treasure, whether in bullion, coin, or precious objects, was unproductive. It could buy a few services, especially the military service of young men and the attention of poets, but it was not a tool that could be easily put to work. The poet Gunnlaug asked permission from King Æthelred to leave his court and recited :

> I must go visit the house of three princes and two earls; this I have promised the possessors of land. I shall not return before the giver of gold summon me. Give the servant of the goddess of the spear-point the red couch of the dragons (gold) for his sleeves.

So Æthelred gave the poet a gold ring that weighed six ounces, and told him to come back next autumn.

In the main, treasure was the spoil of war, loot and tribute. It was the luxury of the ruling classes, something to gloat over, to be generous with, to heap up in treasuries and churches, to display for amazement or envy. And so, although in saga 'the fire of Leifi's road', gold, is the glittering prize, this is because in heroic verse we are in the company of those soldier-heroes, 'the eggers-on of war', 'the partners in the storm of the corpse-fire', whose minds are, for a time, above the mundane cares of life. They fight for pleasure, honour, renown, and special boon. Life is transient but fame endures. As King Hrothgar said to Beowulf, 'By your exploits you have established your fame for ever.' In this society the great lord is often 'the lord of land', but he is one who 'forces his neighbours to submit and pay him tribute', so that for his men he is a bestower of swords, byrnies, and helmets, of horses, and of rings and jewels. He is 'the gracious giver of mighty gifts', 'a gold-giver', 'a scatterer of the ice of the hand', 'the guardian of the soldiers' treasury.' Waker of battle, he breaks the raven's sleep, and leads his men through the bickering of weapons to the reckoning day in his hall.

Yet even in saga there is one feat beyond all others—to win a kingdom, for here was honour and loot and land. In the poem 'Widsith', copied into the Exeter Book about the year 1000 and commemorating the deeds of the heathen heroes of the migration period, Offa king of Angel, the fourth-century ancestor of the kings of Mercia, was remembered because, 'prince of men, he gained while still a youth (*cniht*) the greatest of kingdoms. At Fifeldor (the River Eider) he fixed the boundary against the Myrgingas. No one of his age did greater deeds of valour in battle with his single sword.' The title of king was greatly prized. In the Saga of Olaf Haraldsson King Cnut was jealous of Olaf, whom he had taken into his service, and severely blamed his bishop Sigurth for paying him too much honour. 'Is it true', he asked, 'that you have called Olaf by the title of king this winter? Now how do you defend your words when he has no settled country nor wears a crown?' Sigurth replied, 'It is true, my lord, that he has no land here, and he wears no crown of gold or silver, but he has been chosen by God to rule Norway.'

By the eleventh century there were fewer kings in Europe and royal dignity had become so much the greater. There was a gulf in honour between a duke, count, or earl and a king. In a society where lineage counted for so much, the proudest boast was to be a king who was descended from kings. And in northern Europe the most distinguished royal line was the English, for Edward the Confessor could trace back through about twenty kings to Cerdic, who about the year 519 'succeeded to the kingdom of the West Saxons'.

Moreover by the eleventh century conquest of territory had become less easy. Not many thinly-populated or lightly-defended regions worth the conquering remained. Feudal society, being organized for war and usually engaged in it, was seldom far out of equilibrium. It was rare for a count, a duke, or even a king, using his feudal resources, completely to destroy another feudal grouping, likewise defended by castles and soldiers. Two nations alone were conquerors. The German kings could now and then raise great armies and invade Italy, and take the Italian crown at Pavia and the imperial diadem at Rome. And the Scandinavian peoples, the Vikings, whose ravaging and settlements had been far-flung, achieved their last great successes. There was the conquest of England at the beginning of the eleventh century first by Svein of Denmark and then by his son, Cnut. There was the penetration of Apulia by Norman adventurers in the decades after 1038; and there was Duke William's conquest of England.

In this phase of Scandinavian expansion Cnut, king three times over, obtained the widest rule. But he was overshadowed by the great Norwegian heroes, Olaf Tryggvason and Olaf Haraldsson, and his rise lacked the drama of William's. Moreover the duke had a different and a wider circle of admirers. He was a conqueror whom all—even grudgingly the conquered—could esteem. An orphaned bastard, he won, against the odds, first his father's county and then his cousin's crown and kingdom. To get the crown he defeated and killed his rival in a pitched battle, and, a crowned and anointed king loaded with spoils and proud with hostages, he was back in Normandy within six months of his having set out on campaign. This was a triumph almost without peer. And most could approve. The Northmen in Neustria had become French and much of Gaul had sent some troops to William's army. The church had blessed the expedition, and after the victory William poured out the spoils on the churches. In the decade which followed 1066 there was one of the greatest redistributions of wealth that medieval man could remember. And so, although contemporaries were reluctant to abandon the title of 'the bastard' in favour of something grander, William was soon hailed as *triumphator* and *conquestor*—a successful claimant and thence, with a shift of meaning, a military conqueror—so that in the end his elaborate plea that he had never acquired anything to which he was not entitled by law was hidden by a more ruthless acclaim.

The epitaph written for him by Baudri of Bourgueil in

sedate Latin elegiacs—as remote as could be from the
'kennings' of northern poetry—is typical :

> Who, as the heavenly comet first foretold,
>> Through thickest carnage England won,
> And ruled as duke the Normans, Caesar there,
>> Who poured his wealth as from a spring,
> This William, rich in empire, children, wife,
>> Expired and left them all behind.

We have in fact moved out of the world of saga into
that of the literary epic and romance. In the Saga of
Gunnlaug we read, '(In Æthelred's time) there was the
same speech in England as in Norway and Denmark, but
the speech in England was changed when William the
Bastard won the land. French prevailed in England from
that time forth, since he was French by birth.' William,
the descendant of a line of Viking warriors, was himself
a soldier, but of a feudal kind, a knight, and his soldier-
sons were even more remote in their attitudes from the
Scandinavian tradition. William was basically, totally,
and pre-eminently a *miles*. Like all feudal lords he learned
to fight and then to rule, and the one grew naturally out
of, and was a sort of extension of, the other. He spent all
his life almost exclusively in a military society. William
was more talented than most of his contemporaries and
once he had caught the wind he never got becalmed. But,
although he travelled farther than most, he was in no way
extraordinary. He had no traits, whether physical or of
character, which were unusual, which cannot be paral-
leled in many of his peers, and he gives the impression
of being completely representative of his age.

It is a common fallacy to think that important events
must have had important causes, that great conquests are
necessarily the result of great battles, or that notable
achievements must have involved notable men. It is William's success rather than his genius that is remarkable;
and by studying the life of this princely knight we should
form an idea of a particular eleventh-century feudal culture and see how this was introduced into England after
the Norman conquest and what effects it had on the
ancient insular civilization over which it was spread. The

story is largely of warfare and of the social organization of a military class, a society in which religion had an important place. The *bellatores* and the *oratores* formed an aristocracy over the *laboratores* whose labour produced the wealth which enabled the others to follow their less utilitarian pursuits. It is also a representative story because eleventh-century men, as shown to us by the chroniclers, are little more than types. If they are described, it is in conventional terms, and if they are given motives (which is rare) these are ascribed to the simplest emotions. Their words are seldom quoted in a form which inspires confidence; their thoughts remain hidden from us. Hence their recorded actions are often inexplicable except by an imaginative reconstruction which, in the absence of evidence, is more appropriate to the novel than to the history book. The impossibility of getting securely inside the men and their public deeds should not, however, lead us into the error of regarding this as a puppet world. The writings of an Anselm prove that men were capable of the most subtle thought, and the complexity of the diplomacy shows that rulers were often engaged in cunning political reasoning. The historian can do little more than make his own pattern from the facts which he selects and generalize from his knowledge and experience. But the reader may use a freer imagination.

Chapter One

William's Early Years (1027–1064)

IN the year 1027 or 1028 Herleva, the young daughter of Fulbert, a burgess and tanner of Falaise, gave birth to a son. Her lover, Robert, the equally young son of Count Richard II of Normandy, had taken her as his mistress while he had been ruling the Hiémois as a subordinate during the short principality of his elder brother, Count Richard III. Herleva bore him two children, this boy, William, and a daughter, Adelaide.

Norman sexual morals were loose even by the standards of the time. Christian marriage, because it was binding and controlled by the church, was often shirked in favour of marriages in the Scandinavian manner, unions contracted without the blessing of the church, for these could be continued or superseded when it was necessary to marry according to Christian rites for reasons of state. It was also usual to keep concubines. From a strictly ecclesiastical standpoint many members of the ruling family in Normandy were of doubtful legitimacy. But society would not extend its usual tolerance to the children of Robert and Herleva. William was so regularly called a bastard (*nothus, bastardus*) that it became almost a surname. This exceptional contempt was due to several factors. Robert seems to have made provision for Herleva before he went on pilgrimage in 1034 by marrying her to his servant and vassal, Herlwin, *vicomte* of Conteville. If Robert had indeed already married, and repudiated, Estrith, the sister of Cnut, king of England, there was little else that he could have done for Herleva. All the same, his action branded her as a concubine, and at a time when the church's pressure against irregular unions was increasing. By 1028 some of the clergy no longer minced their words : William was a bastard; and the term *nothus* was particularly apt, for, according to Isidore's *Etymologiae* (I, vii), it means someone born of unlike, or imperfectly matched, stock. There was also the disappointment and anger felt by most members of the ruling family when Count Robert appointed William as his heir. For them, too, the boy was a bastard. Their scorn is understandable. Herleva bore an honourable Germanic name and Robert's uncle, Robert, archbishop of Rouen and count of Évreux, was married—as count—to her namesake. But in the parvenu aristocracy of Normandy social cleavages were becoming sharper. And it was in the obvious interest of the other claimants to the county to stress William's illegitimacy.

William, however, was not born of a casual or loveless encounter. He became close to his mother's kin and intimate with his step-brothers, Odo and Robert. It was to Herleva and Herlwin that his own bride, Matilda of Flanders, was delivered by the count her father; and it was their younger son, Robert, count of Mortain and a great lord in England, who was with him when he died.

About the time of William's birth his father succeeded to the whole duchy of Normandy on the death of Richard III. Although the chronology is uncertain and disputed, the weight of the evidence seems to be slightly inclined to 1027 for Robert's accession and to 1028 for William's birth. If this was so, William had one advantage to set against his bastardy, for, according to the ideas of the time, a son born while his father ruled, also assumed a worthiness to rule.

When Robert had governed Normandy for eight years, he decided to go on a pilgrimage to Jerusalem. His government had been disturbed by the conspiracies of kinsmen but had not been unsuccessful. His sins do not seem to have been extraordinary. And the rumour that he had poisoned his brother in order to succeed was probably invented by enemies to cheapen his piety. Pilgrimages to Jerusalem were common enough in the early eleventh century. Fulk, count of Anjou, went at least twice. In 1026 the count of Angoulême led a party to Jerusalem. Travelling overland they left at the beginning of October, reached their destination in March, and were back towards the end of June. Robert also conducted a party; and it is best to regard his action as no more than a slightly extravagant religious gesture which would have aroused admiration rather than amazement.

These journeys, although most survived them, had their dangers, and it was considered prudent to make a will before setting out. Robert made his dispositions for the future. He persuaded the Norman barons to accept his only son, the bastard William, now seven or eight years old, as his heir, and he secured the approval of his feudal superior, Henry I, king of France, for the arrangement. But a settlement which was probably regarded by all as provisional—for there was still plenty of time for Robert to regularize his matrimonial position and beget a legitimate heir—became irrevocable and final when Robert died on the return journey from Jerusalem in June 1035. He had gone out through Constantinople and was soon on his way back. He had almost reached Constantinople again when he died at Nicaea and was buried by his companions in the church of St Mary within the walls. According to William of Malmesbury, King William towards the end of his life sent men to Nicaea to bring back his father's body; but these, surprised in Apulia by the news of their master's death, buried Robert there.

Feudal society, although always irked by strong government, showed no enthusiasm for the rule of a child. The advantage of freedom from control had to be balanced against the certainty of disorder and injustice and the likelihood of external danger. There would be no one to protect the weak against the strong and the whole country against the depredations of neighbours. Had there been available in 1035 a suitable adult male of the ruling house doubtless Robert's arrangement would have been upset in his favour. But there was none. Among the many descendants of Count Richard I there was no one who was not disqualified by holy orders, illegitimacy, other allegiance, or inability to secure general support. William was accepted as count of Normandy and all men prepared themselves for the inevitable lack of government.

The French county, to which William had unexpectedly succeeded, had been formed out of the areas conquered and colonized by the Northmen, the Vikings, in north-west Gaul during the ninth and tenth centuries. King Charles III (the Simple) had made an agreement with one of the invaders, Rolf or Rollo, apparently a Norwegian, granting him at Saint-Clair-sur-Epte in 911 the city of Rouen and its neighbourhood, especially perhaps the land in the angle between the Rivers Epte and Seine. He seems to have appointed him as a marcher-lord to keep the other Scandinavians at bay. But Rolf and his descendants extended their authority over all the Viking settlements in the area and created a lordship which became a real political entity. They assumed, or were allowed, the title of count, which besides indicating their subordination to the king also gave them legitimate governmental powers. In 965 at Gisors on the Epte King Lothair recognized Count Richard I's rule over the Bessin, the Cotentin, and the Avranchin. The boundaries of Normandy were thus determined in a general way (feudal lordships rarely had sharp frontiers) a century before the Norman conquest of England. Starting from the Channel in the north, they ran up the River Bresle from Eu to Aumale, across to the Epte, and so to the Seine, then south-westerly to include Mortagne and Alençon, and so westerly to march with the county of Brittany. The crescent shape of the county is that of an extended beach-head; but it also corresponds roughly with the old Roman province of *Lugdunensis Secunda*, which gave form to the ecclesiastical province of Rouen. These ancient boundaries possibly facilitated Viking expansion within them and certainly compensated for the lack of obvious natural frontiers.

Normandy was also kept in shape by the pressure of its neighbours. To the north was the county of Flanders (with the county of Ponthieu as the march), to the east the duchy of France (under the Capetian kings, royal demesne), to the south-east and south the counties of Chartres and Blois and the county of Anjou (with the county of Maine in dispute), and to the south-west Brittany. The Norman counts claimed, without much historical justification, that both Brittany and Maine had been put under their lordship by French kings. In fact by military pressure and marriage alliances they succeeded in exerting an intermittent influence over Brittany, similar to that of the English kings over Wales. Maine, more essential than Brittany to the safety and ambitions of Anjou, presented quite different problems.

Thus the Northmen in France, unlike their fellow settlers in England, created a principality, and although Normandy after 987 bordered on an important area of royal demesne, the kings of France had no wish to destroy this new lordship. France was composed almost entirely of similar duchies and counties, and all that the kings desired was to obtain the homage and fealty and the obedience of the dukes and counts. It may be that the count of Normandy was from the beginning, and thereafter usually, the vassal of the French king, and that the king regarded him as enfeoffed with his county or with its lands. But, characteristic of the period, the strands in the relationship appear confused, and, of course, the relationship itself changed according to circumstances. What is clear is that the kings seldom required from the counts much more than loyalty and military support and that the counts, exercising the powers of their office and, like other counts, usurping more, were allowed to appoint *vicomtes* (deputy-counts) and bishops, coin money, and hold courts from which there was no regular appeal to the king. Despite their pride and virtual autonomy the counts became remarkably loyal vassals to the kings of France; and there was established a tradition that each should help the other in case of need. From the accession of Hugh Capet as king in 987 until 1052 the official and feudal relationship was warmed by an alliance based on common interests.

As the counts ruled like petty kings we notice in the eleventh century a move to inflate their style. To the English chroniclers the count was an earl, to the Scandinavians the jarl of Rouen. William of Poitiers, when writing his book about William the Bastard's deeds in 1073–4, used the titles *comes* (count), *dux* (duke), and *princeps* (ruler, or prince) indifferently, and Orderic Vital, who finished his *Historia Ecclesiastica* before 1141, often refers to him as *marchio* (marquis). The title *dux Normannorum* was applied easily by writers describing the military exploits of that nation, for the count was usually the *dux* or general. It is possible that William, although he often appears as *comes* in documents, preferred the title of duke, and for the sake of consistency we will use it here.

The counts of Normandy had an adequate material basis for their power. Normandy, like England which it resembles, has good soils and a favourable climate, and in the eleventh century was a fairly prosperous area of France. The exploitation of the county's natural resources, however, had been hindered by the Viking devastation followed by endemic disorder. And Normandy, although divided by the navigable Seine and traversed by important roads, was off the main arteries of European trade. Rouen seems to have been a busy city and port; Caen, and perhaps some other towns, grew in size under William's rule; but in Normandy, unlike Flanders which was geographically much better placed, there was no incentive to the development of handicrafts for a wide market. Minted coin seems to have been less plentiful in Normandy than in England. There was potential wealth : the many abbeys founded in William's time and the many churches rebuilt represent a large capital investment, and the counts themselves seem never to have been financially embarrassed. They were, to be sure, princes who kept little state. They were richer than the counts of Brittany and perhaps many of their peers; but the wealth the Normans found in England was to intoxicate them for a generation.

The Vikings, after all allowances have been made for their artistic skill, interest in law and trade, and social ability, were more primitive in culture than the southern peoples whom they conquered. And although the problem of what they accepted and what they contributed is still debated for each of their conquests, no historian would now take the extreme view that they wantonly destroyed the institutions they found in order to substitute their own. The Viking settlements in Gaul were chaotic for a time, but it was not an isolated area, and the Normans were soon influenced both by the people they settled among and by travellers through the county. Rolf and his successors learned to behave as counts and preserved much of the old administrative framework, and the Normans as they became French acquired Frankish feudalism and Christianity.

Feudalism, like similar terms such as capitalism and communism, is a rather vague descriptive concept. Even when restricted to describe conditions between the Rivers Loire and Rhine from the ninth to, say, the thirteenth century, it still has to embrace a large number of regional differences and, of course, the often rapid changes which took place over the years. We shall return to this difficulty in Chapter Seven when we discuss the introduction of Norman customs into England after the Conquest. The word, however, exists and is in common use; and some of the social and economic phenomena regarded as peculiar to feudalism are these : within the free classes there were lords and vassals, a private not a public arrangement of authority. Socially there was a grouping of soldiers round their lord, bound by the oath of fealty and the doing of homage, and close-knit through the ethics of a military society which believed in courage and loyalty. Economically the vassals were maintained directly by their lord or by the revenues of the land which he had loaned them (the *beneficium*, benefice, or *feudum*, fief—hence 'feudal'); while the lords lived off their demesne and used the services—mainly military—of their vassals.

The Vikings had already been organized in military groups governed by a code of honour, and feudal customs could easily develop among them. There is always a heavy mortality among a military aristocracy, and the feudal baronage of 1066, the families which were to make their fortunes in England, arose in the years after 1000, and was largely the creation of Counts Richard II (996–1026) and Robert (1027–35), although some of William's friends owed their advancement mainly to him and benefited from the destruction or crippling of older families in the anarchy, rebellions, and wars after 1035. The counts endowed their favourites more with confiscations from other nobles and the church, especially decayed monasteries, than with land taken from their own demesne. Since feudal customs were still developing and had not reached the legal precision of later centuries, we do not know the exact terms on which these benefices were granted; but we can see that the early counts were unable to enforce or enlarge the duties of their vassals. The history of Normandy in the period before 1053 proves that the most vital feudal groups were formed by the barons and their own military vassals, men living mostly close together and often going out to fight against the forces of another lord. Much more frail, because less intimate, was the bond between these barons and the count. Occasionally they attended his court, sometimes they accompanied him on campaign; but often they were independent and unresponsive, and now and then they rebelled. There was certainly no ideal 'feudal system' in Normandy.

Organized Christianity had almost disappeared from the region when Rolf accepted baptism in 911 and more than half a century was to pass before substantial progress had been made in restoring the devastated and often deserted abbeys and cathedral churches. Count Richard I (942–96) and, more successfully, his son, Richard II (996–1026), initiated or encouraged the restoration of monasteries; and after Mainard, a disciple of Gerard of Broigne, left Ghent for Normandy in 961 and William of Volpiano—or of Dijon—arrived in 1001 the monastic movement, thus enriched by both Flemish and Cluniac reform, gathered pace. Norman monasticism, which was revived effectively about a generation after the similar reform in England, never perhaps before 1066 reached the cultural heights attained in the kingdom; but it probably preserved its moral tone better and longer. In the more primitive, in a way more barbarous—certainly more disorderly and violent—county the spiritual aims of monasticism remained precious for some time after zeal had begun to cool in the more sophisticated kingdom. The counts were the patrons of all the monasteries founded before 1030, and this patronage, although severe in economic and administrative affairs, was usually enlightened in religious matters.

The ecclesiastical hierarchy also was re-established. The ecclesiastical province of Rouen, largely coterminous with the county, contained six dioceses, with bishops in the cities of Évreux, Lisieux, Bayeux, Coutances, Avranches, and Séez. All these bishoprics, except the last, which was

in the fief and under the patronage of the count of Bellême, were under the direct control of the count of Normandy, who usually appointed kinsmen to them. Hence
the Norman bishops, as belonging to the high aristocracy,
rarely lacked vigour and ambition. A few were even good
men; but as a class they were not deeply interested in the
spiritual life. There was a cleavage between the episcopate
and the abbeys, which was indeed common enough on the
Continent, but which was unlike the position in England.

By the eleventh century the Normans were coming to
be accepted as but one more of the 'nations' in France.
They were still regarded with some reserve by the more
ancient and civilized peoples, but it was evident that they
had become French, had adopted many of the current
fashions, and were only distinguished from other nations
by those small peculiarities which are so difficult to define
yet always arouse interest. Although national characters
are usually caricatures it would not be unfair to describe
the Norman nobility as exceptionally rough and fierce
and, when touched by religion, outstandingly pious. They
had a passion for fighting and hunting and deservedly enjoyed a high reputation as soldiers. A simple hard life,
uncorrupted by social graces, produced courage, endurance, and resourcefulness. They were adventurous and
always ready, like their forbears, for a raid or expedition,
however far afield. And they were adaptable, able to in-
filtrate among other peoples and settle down happily in
the strangest conditions if the opportunity offered and
pleased.

Yet although they were resourceful there is no evidence
that they were inventive or politically gifted. It is difficult to point to any aspect of Norman culture which was
purely Scandinavian in origin. Such art—except possibly
in woodwork—and learning as they acquired came from
beneath or without. Their social and political customs
seem to be essentially those of their neighbours. They soon
regarded the Bretons as different, an attitude which im-
plied that they themselves observed common form. And although, in view of their governmental success in England,
they have often been credited with administrative talent,
the political history of Normandy lends no support to this

view. Except during the rule of a few exceptional men Normandy was generally turbulent; and the government of the counts and barons was primitive. No doubt there were customs and institutions capable of development—and William made some progress—but the comital administration, which may well have been in advance of common French practice, was rudimentary by the standards of the Eastern Empire, Germany, or England. The Normans were happiest when engaged in physical action; and since their pursuits were dangerous they were a religious people. Norman soldiers were often extravagant in their appeals to God and the saints to preserve their lives and give them victory in battle. And as the savagery of war sometimes aroused in the end a sense of guilt it was not rare in Normandy for an old warrior to make generous amends to the church or even to renounce the world and become a monk. In short, the Normans pushed to extremes attitudes which were common in the feudal society of the period.

All contemporaries agree that the Normans were hard to govern. They needed a ruler even fiercer than themselves. While William was a boy, from 1035 until after 1042, there was no effective central government in Normandy. His great-uncle, Archbishop Robert of Rouen, until his death in 1037, gave him valuable support; but the next archbishop, Mauger, William's uncle, was less disinterested. Count Robert had appointed as guardians to his son two of his own cousins, Alan III, count of Brittany, and Gilbert, count of Brionne, and a more distant kinsman, Osbern, his seneschal or steward. All three died a violent death before William grew up, and the boy's tutor also was murdered. Little is clear from the confused accounts of this period given us by later chroniclers except that William, protected by his mother's family and a few loyal vassals and servants, was lucky to have survived the collapse of law and order.

Feudal lords took over ducal castles and threw up their own to defend their estates, and then made war on each other. Some recruited soldiers from France. There was assassination with consequent blood feuds. There were plots and treachery. William himself was scarcely involved directly in this turmoil, which must be regarded more as a withdrawal of fealty from the count than as a conspiracy against him. But his guardians got caught up in it, and there was always the danger that William would fall with one of his protectors. The county itself was largely spared from attack owing to the preoccupation of its neighbours. Alan of Brittany was busy as a guardian and when he died in 1040 his son and heir, Conan II, was a child. The old Fulk Nerra of Anjou also died in 1040 after years of trouble with his son, Geoffrey Martel, a fine soldier who had been making war against Aquitaine and was soon to turn against Blois and Chartres. According to the Norman chroniclers the most hostile was the man most bound to keep the peace and protect his ward and vassal's interests, William's overlord, King Henry. But although it is possible that the king could not resist getting some advantage from the governmental collapse, it is likely that most of his interventions were in William's favour and were misconstrued later. William reached his fifteenth year in 1042. It was about then that he was knighted and began to play a more independent part in the affairs of his county.

William's character must have been moulded by these experiences. His bastardy, always a taunt available to his enemies, may well have inspired his implacable ambition. It may also have given him a dislike of sexual immorality. He became a persecutor of immoral and married clerks. His earliest admirers do not praise the chastity of his life —and with William of Poitiers, who wrote so much about his hero's moral and religious qualities, the omission is significant. But he married young, and only once, and is not known to have fathered any child outside that marriage. Outwardly at least his private life was respectable; and by the twelfth century there was some speculation about this feature, so unusual among princes of the time. William's morals are discussed by William of Malmesbury. He reports that William's abstinence as a young man gave rise to a rumour of impotence, and he cites one alleged example of William's marital infidelity, but only to cast doubt on it. Malmesbury is possibly right. There could well have been a puritanical side to William's character. But when we remember that homosexuality was rife in monastic and military circles, that William's favourite son, Rufus, was notorious in this respect, and that the fourth son, Henry, was distinctly abnormal, it may be that William, like Edward the Confessor, simply had no great interest in women.

Probably even more influential on William's character than his illegitimate birth were the perils and treacheries of his boyhood. His schooling was probably more utilitarian than was general even in that uncultured age. He was completely illiterate and never showed more than a bandit's interest in any work of art. He was trained as a soldier. He learned the art of war in a hard school. He learned to survive in a society riddled with intrigue and deceit. His experiences made him a man who believed in guile, failing which, force. He was distrustful and secretive and gave his confidence to few whom he had not known long and tested extensively—especially the friends of his boyhood. He hated disorder and schism and was authoritarian in every aspect of life. Early insecurity gave him a love of wealth and power. Some of these traits were probably only just emerging in 1042–3, some were modified by later experiences; others were added. At the age of fifteen he was ready to fight for his inheritance, to recover the rights lost since his father's death. He was an eager knight.

William's first attempts to rule inevitably irritated the nobility and especially ducal servants who had become unaccustomed to control. In 1046, when he was approaching nineteen, a serious rebellion broke out in western Normandy. The leader of the revolt was a possible claimant to the county, William's cousin, Guy, the second son of the count of Burgundy, and in Normandy count of Brionne and Vernon, a young man who had been a boyhood companion of his lord and who held Brionne through his special gift. He was supported by two important officials, Nigel, *vicomte* of the Cotentin, and Ranulf, *vicomte* of Bayeux, and by many other nobles. William was powerless against this formidable league and fled from Normandy to appeal to his overlord for help. In 1047 King Henry invaded the Hiémois and, together with William, met the rebels at Val-des-dunes, south-east of Caen, put them to rout, and drove many of them into the River Arne. After the victory Henry returned home and William besieged Brionne which capitulated after a long blockade. William was not yet strong enough to punish the defeated nobles. But he took hostages and ordered many castles to be thrown down. He had provoked a rebellion and defeated it, and was able to take constructive measures towards reducing disorder. What is more, he was already displaying military qualities which became characteristic. We notice his prudence in securing sufficient aid and his determination and patience in completing the defeat of a rival. And although we do not have to believe with the duke's panegyrist, William of Poitiers, that the Norman won the day, with a little help from the king, almost single-handed we can assume that he fought bravely in his first pitched battle.

The siege of Brionne, situated almost in the centre of Normandy, may have lasted until the end of 1049, and during those years William was obviously most insecure. The last important rebellion against the duke was suppressed in 1053, and it was not before 1060 that he emerged as a real power in northern France. After Val-des-dunes William also gradually became involved in diplomacy and warfare with his neighbours. At first he probably followed the lead of the king and it is difficult to say when he began to form his own plans and to what extent he ever developed a conscious 'foreign' policy. Certainly before 1060 he appears to have been more often the victim of circumstance than the master of his destiny. As soon as he began to operate outside his duchy he increased his risks, for internal malcontents were given possible allies and the chance of taking advantage of a ducal defeat. And, no less important, there began that hostility between Normandy and Anjou, and the dispute over Maine, which was to trouble William throughout his life and plague his descendants until 1154, when Henry II, duke of Normandy as well as count of Anjou, succeeded Stephen in England.

The county of Anjou was no more ancient than Normandy, which it resembled in many ways. The ancestors of the ruling house had originally been *vicomtes* of Angers, officials of those Robertian counts who became in turn dukes and, after 987, the Capetian kings of France; and step by step, through the elevation of their lords, the *vicomtes* advanced to be counts under a duke and then immediate vassals of the king. The new Angevin counts were as fierce and ambitious as the Norman. Hitherto they had tried to extend their territory north-east into Touraine and Blois and southwards into Poitou rather than into Normandy, being satisfied with lordship over Maine. But the Normans themselves had claims to that buffer county and were anxious to get the homage of its counts in order to be in a position to exert more pressure on Brittany and also prevent Angevin interference in that politically unstable region.

The general political situation in north-west Europe after 1047 was largely determined by the Lotharingian rebellion against the Emperor Henry III, in which Baldwin of Flanders (1035–67) was implicated. Baldwin was supported by his brother-in-law, Henry, king of France, and the emperor was in alliance with Edward, king of England, and Geoffrey Martel, count of Anjou. In the period 1047–53 William did some things which largely shaped his future career. He began his wars with Anjou; he allied with England and Flanders; and he incurred the enmity of the king of France. Few of these events can be dated exactly; but William of Poitiers gives them in a sequence which should be accepted until it can be proved wrong.

When William first attacked Anjou, probably within the period 1048–50, he was merely serving his king. Geoffrey of Anjou had captured and imprisoned Theobald III of Blois and Chartres in 1044 during the struggle for Touraine, and in the winter of 1047–8 had captured Gervase, bishop of Le Mans. King Henry was exasperated by these actions of his unruly vassal and led an army, which included at least the duty forces of Normandy and Blois–Chartres, against the Angevin town of Mouliherne. William seems to have revelled in the fighting. It was his first important subordinate command, and he was clearly hard to control. He delighted in small-scale raids and scouting expeditions with his own knights. On one occasion his forces mistook Theobald's contingent for the

enemy and almost gave battle. William increased his reputation as a soldier. Poitiers even claims that his opponent
graciously admitted that he was the finest knight in the
world and allows that only one reproach was made against
his conduct by his wiser seniors : he was too rash and ex-
posed himself unnecessarily to danger.

At about the same time, in or before 1049, when he was
twenty-one, William made his first recorded diplomatic
move. He opened negotiations with Baldwin V of Flanders
for the hand of his daughter, Matilda. It may be that
King Henry persuaded his vassal to join the alliance.
Possibly William had motives of his own. William cannot
be allowed much military or diplomatic importance in
1049, especially if we place his main campaign against
Anjou after that year, but his intervention in European
diplomacy provoked a lively reaction. The emperor was
displeased that Baldwin was making friends, and the
emperor's ally, Pope Leo IX, at the council of Rheims in
October 1049, forbade the marriage, presumably on the
grounds of consanguinity. Yet so anxious was William for
an alliance with Flanders that before the end of 1053,
possibly in 1052 after the Domfront and Alençon campaign, he married Matilda despite the papal ban, and
incurred some ecclesiastical censure.

As William almost certainly did not marry for love—it
is unlikely that he had ever seen his betrothed before she
was delivered to his representatives—his tenacity in
making the Flemish treaty despite the obstacles and risks
proves how much he valued it. In the first place he was
marrying a little above him—William of Poitiers is elo-
quent over the distinction of the bride's descent—and the
attraction for a bastard of a distinguished marriage cannot
be disregarded. But we must also think that William was
extending his influence in a direction in which he wanted
to go. We notice that he arranged marriages for his sister,
Adelaide, in the same area. Not later than 1052 she
married Enguerrand, count of Ponthieu and lord of
Aumale, on the northern frontier of the duchy. When
Enguerrand was killed before Arques in 1053, she married
Lambert, count of Lens in Artois, younger brother of
Count Eustace II of Boulogne. Eustace was married to

Godgifu, Edward the Confessor's sister, the daughter of King Æthelred and Emma of Normandy. Adelaide was again widowed in 1054 when Lambert was killed in battle at Lille. Thirdly, but perhaps some time later, she married Odo, who had been deprived by his uncle of the county of Champagne. William's interest in his northern marches is remarkable. And this brings us to his relations with England, a difficult subject because we have little more than the Norman official version of the diplomacy, published, even if not composed, some years after the Conquest.

William of Poitiers, the count's biographer, had as one of his main purposes in writing his book the justification of William's conquests. His general theme is that William, a paragon of virtue, never engaged in an unjust war; and accordingly he demonstrates the legality and moral justification of William's behaviour towards King Harold and England. He made use, it seems, of a tractate which the duke's advisers composed probably in 1066 to use in diplomacy with the pope and other European powers. According to this thesis, Edward, because of his kinship to William, the many benefits that he and his family had received from the Norman dukes, and William's suitability as an ally and successor, appointed William his heir. This act was taken with the consent of the English *witan*, who swore to uphold it, and was reinforced by the giving of hostages by Godwin, earl of Wessex. As we are also informed that Robert, archbishop of Canterbury, was Edward's agent in the business, its date must be 1050–1. One English chronicler believed that William actually visited England in 1051–2 (although this is impossible if the duke was besieging Domfront at that time), and there is no doubt that Eustace, count of Boulogne, a vassal of the count of Flanders and Edward's brother-in-law, made a visit to Edward's court in the autumn of 1051. It is also of interest that Godwin's third son, Tostig, married the sister of the count of Flanders at about the same time.

There is no great difficulty in interpreting these facts, or alleged facts, from William's point of view. Edward was still childless after seventeen years of marriage to a younger woman, and no obvious heir to the English throne was within sight. Edward's mother, Emma, who did not die until 1052, was William's great-aunt, and it must have seemed to the duke that his claim on hereditary grounds to succeed Edward was not much worse than those which could be put forward by all the others related to Æthelred or Cnut. At all events we can assume that he had begun to get into position for pressing his claim when Edward died. By creating a maritime alliance with Baldwin of Flanders, possibly Eustace and then Lambert of Boulogne, and Godwin, earl of Wessex, he placed himself as well as he could; and he must have thought that this situation was worth the possible dangers he was running. William may indeed have had an important short-term interest in a treaty with England. The emperor had secured English naval support against Flanders in 1049 and William may have wished to neutralize that threat.

Far less clear are Edward's attitude and intentions. The Norman thesis that he wished to repay a debt of gratitude to the Norman court and that his constant desire was to have William as his heir is almost certainly a simplification. Edward and his brother and sister had been taken by their mother, Queen Emma, to seek refuge with her Norman kinsmen in 1013 when the Danish invasion of England reached its climax. But between 1017, when Emma married her first husband's supplanter, Cnut, until 1035, when Cnut died, the Norman court had kept Edward out of what he could have regarded as his inheritance. It is possible that Count Robert, just before he left for the Holy Land, threatened Cnut in Edward's interests, and Edward may have received some Norman aid for the expedition he led to England in 1035–6; but when he finally returned to his native land in 1041 William was only fourteen years old and in no position to help him. It must have been Edward's mother who called him back to replace Harthacnut, her son by Cnut, who was close to his premature death. And Edward was so ungrateful for these tardy amends that as soon as he was crowned king in 1043 he led some of the great earls to Winchester to despoil his mother of her treasures as punishment for neglecting his interests. That mother and son were soon reconciled is no proof that it then became Edward's desire to advance his other Norman kinsmen. We have only the assertion of William of Poitiers that Edward loved William as a brother or son, and it is easy to believe that, even if Edward had been fond of his young cousin, a decade's separation must have cooled the affection.

It is easier to explain Edward's actions from the standpoint of his own and his kingdom's interests. England's standing problem was the hostility of Flanders which could be used as an advanced base by the Vikings and as a harbour by English malcontents. The usual answer was an alliance with Normandy. From 1043 until 1051 Edward could probably rely on Normandy's benevolence through the influence of his mother. And in this period he was in alliance with the Emperor Henry III against Baldwin of Flanders. Therefore, when William allied with Flanders in 1049 Edward was placed in a perilous position. If we accept the Norman thesis that the offer of the succession to the English throne was indeed made by Edward, we can probably interpret it as an attempt to buy off this danger. William could have blackmailed Edward into the grant. Generally speaking the Anglo-Norman alliance was probably as advantageous to England as to Normandy and it was doubtless recognized as such among the English magnates. It promised peace from marauders in the Channel and indeed secured it until 1066. At the same time we need not take the promise of the succession, whether voluntary or extorted, too seriously. To be able to dangle a crown before pretenders was a wonderful diplomatic asset to a childless king. William's future cannot have appeared secure in 1050. Svein Estrithson, king of Denmark, maintained that he too had been made Edward's heir. After 1054 Edward negotiated in Germany and Hungary for the return of English princes who had been exiled by Cnut. Diplomatic promises are made to be broken. All the same, William was possibly moving in a chosen direction and beginning to assemble a case.

It was probably immediately after the negotiations with England and while the talks with Flanders proceeded that William engaged in his second and more serious campaign against Anjou. And it is unlikely that this war was of William's choosing. On 26 March 1051 Hugh IV, count of

Maine, died. Geoffrey of Anjou occupied the county and then threatened Normandy by taking two castles, Domfront and Alençon, which had been enfeoffed by the Norman counts to the family of Bellême, an important family whose possessions, held of various lords, were strung along the borders of Normandy from the Vexin to Brittany. William's court had become an asylum for refugees from Maine, Hugh's widow, Bertha, and her children, Herbert II and Margaret, and Bishop Gervase of Le Mans, now released from captivity. Moreover, his faithful vassal, Roger of Montgomery, *vicomte* of the Hiémois, had married, or was about to marry, Mabel, the chief heiress to the family of Bellême. William naturally made Roger's cause his own, for a loyal man was required in that doubtful area.

It is unlikely that Geoffrey had any designs on Normandy itself. But William reacted sharply. He invested Domfront by constructing four castles, and for a time enjoyed the ambushes and sorties which enliven a siege. When all was quiet he hunted. Once, when he went to ravage for supplies, and his movements were betrayed to the castellan, he was attacked from the rear by a larger force, but turned and chased back the soldiers to the castle. The garrison was quite secure and was merely waiting to be relieved by the count of Anjou. As Geoffrey's army approached, William sent out Roger of Montgomery and William fitzOsbern, his steward, to reconnoitre. Whether William had indeed decided to stand and fight—as William of Poitiers maintains—we do not know. In fact he was relieved of the decision when King Henry pushed into Touraine in support, presumably at William's request, and forced Geoffrey to switch his attention to this more dangerous probe. William, given a free hand, left Domfront besieged and darted through the night against Alençon. Some of the inhabitants of the town called out, 'The tanner! The tanner!' and thumped on hides as the Normans approached. William set fire to the place, took the town, and had the feet and hands of the jokers amputated in full view of the castle. The ferocity persuaded the garrison to surrender. Domfront, equally impressed, gave in too. William pushed a little into Maine and raised a castle at Ambrières, then returned to Rouen.

As William of Poitiers omits from his account the notorious 'pollarding' at Alençon we may be sure that even by contemporary standards William's behaviour was considered barbarous. It is moreover possible that Norman tradition censored an even uglier story, for hides were usually spread on ramparts for protection, especially against fire. That the Norman soldiery loved torches the fate of some Breton and English towns was to prove. William's light-hearted chivalry had already turned sour. He was a man who learned the lessons of the world almost too quickly. He was now aware that a short blaze of ferocity could achieve as much as years of conventional fighting. Poitiers often draws attention to William's mercy. But we can see that clemency or harshness was for his hero a matter of politics. To be sure, once he had shown that he could be terrible a useful impression had been made which did not need frequent repetition; and William could usually control his passions. But men now knew that there was a devil in him and treated him more warily.

It was after this campaign, according to Poitiers, probably as part of the marriage contract, that William secured from his Norman barons oaths of fealty to him as duke and to his heir as yet unborn. Baldwin of Flanders no doubt wished to be sure that he was giving his daughter to a man firmly in the saddle, and that the descent of the county was limited to the issue of the marriage. It was, indeed, William's purpose to found a dynasty. It is perhaps not merely because of his religion that he contracted a Christian marriage relatively young—he would be twenty-five in 1052. He was making sure that, unlike his father and his cousin Edward, he would produce legitimate heirs. And the marriage was fruitful. Four sons—Robert (the future duke of Normandy), Richard (who died young), William Rufus (his father's successor in England), and Henry (Rufus' successor)—and probably more daughters were born over a period of about sixteen years. When Baldwin died in 1067 his hopes had been exceeded. He was to be the grandfather of kings.

William's successes in 1051–2 were outstanding, but the

heavy reverses which followed were a warning against *hubris*. At Domfront, possibly in the winter of 1051-2, William of Arques, an important baron, abandoned his duke and before 15 August 1052 King Henry and Geoffrey of Anjou made peace. This diplomatic revolution may have been unconnected with any of William's actions—Henry may simply have become tired of his struggle with Anjou—but it may easily have been facilitated by William's ambitious plans. Henry was becoming disturbed by the increasing power and independence of his vassal and former ally; he henceforth took advantage of, even if he did not incite, every rebellion in Normandy and was able to associate William's neighbours in this policy. We learn that, besides Geoffrey, Theobald of Blois and Chartres and William VII, duke of Aquitaine and count of Poitou, supported the king. Brittany, under the regent, Eudo of Porhoët, count of Penthièvre, and after 1055 his nephew, Count Conan II, was again hostile. Norman chroniclers writing after the Conquest regarded the French and their king as the constant and implacable enemies of the Normans. But this was a view based only on short periods of recent history—the situation after 1070 and the events of 1053-60.

William was dismayed by Henry's desertion in 1052. He was without effective outside allies. We hear of no help from Flanders, Boulogne, or Ponthieu. Boulogne sheltered exiles from Normandy and the counts of Ponthieu actively helped Norman rebels. The political situation cannot be fully explained; but it should be remembered that all these northern counts were also Henry's vassals and that Baldwin was the king's brother-in-law as well. Feudal loyalties were rarely clear-cut. In any case after 1053 Baldwin was fully occupied with his new rebellion against the emperor. In retrospect it appears that William fought off his enemies if not easily at least with confidence. The attacks from outside were largely punitive and disruptive in purpose and, owing to the loyalty of the greater part of the county to its duke and the strength of the forces which William was always able to collect, never achieved the dislocation intended. But at the time William probably thought that he was fighting for his life and lands.

First there was the threat of the loss of all Normandy beyond the Seine. During the duke's campaign against Domfront, his uncle, William of Arques, count of Talou, deserted and rebelled, and probably obtained at least the sympathy of his brother, Mauger, archbishop of Rouen. Both these men had taken advantage of the minority to increase their power. William of Arques had married the sister of his northern neighbour, Enguerrand of Ponthieu, and may well have had the ambition to turn his fief into a marcher principality, like Bellême. The duke's alliance with Flanders seems to have been the cause of the rebellion. The count of Talou may have thought that he was in danger of being crushed between the contracting powers; and we are told that Mauger opposed the marriage. The rebellion was all the more dangerous because the lands of William of Arques marched with French royal demesne. King Henry had not only the interest but also the opportunity to invade.

In 1053 William invested Arques, and, although Henry broke the blockade in October and supplied the garrison with soldiers and provisions, the fortress was eventually starved out. During the skirmishing an important invader, the count of Ponthieu, was killed. When Arques fell, the duke offered his uncle terms which apparently he refused, preferring exile in the county of Boulogne. In 1054, or possibly 1055, the duke secured the deposition of Archbishop Mauger. This uncle he banished to Guernsey.

Henry's incursion in 1053 was only to annoy. The next year he invaded with his feudal army which included contingents from the duchy of Aquitaine and the county of Burgundy, and perhaps from Anjou under Geoffrey in person. Henry divided his forces into two. He himself entered the county of Évreux and marched on Rouen. William accepted this threat. The second army, under the king's younger brother, Odo, and including Guy count of Ponthieu, who had succeeded after his brother's death before Arques, advanced north of the Seine. It was engaged at Mortemer by Robert, count of Eu, and the northern barons and defeated. A notable captive was Guy, count of Ponthieu. When William informed Henry of this victory the king began to withdraw. Because of the prisoners William drew two advantages from the campaign. The count of Ponthieu became his vassal, and so the duke again increased his influence in the marches of Flanders. And the king seems to have agreed that he would not intervene if William attacked Anjou.

Between 1054 and 1060 William made little headway against Anjou. His penetration of Maine in 1054 was severely punished in 1057 when Henry of France and Geoffrey of Anjou made a deeper and more dangerous push into Normandy. Invading the Hiémois from the south they cut right across the duchy and ravaged the coastal area to the west of the Orne. William apparently could do no more than watch. But when the invading army, while crossing the mouth of the Dives at Varaville, was caught by the tide, William fell on the isolated rear and destroyed it. A desultory and indecisive war followed. It is clear that before the deaths of the French king and the count of Anjou, both in 1060, William was no more than holding his own, and several times received more punishment than he gave. He does, however, seem to have been fairly systematically destroying his internal dynastic rivals. About 1056 he broke his kinsman William Guerlenc, count of Mortain, whom he accused of plotting to rebel, and drove him to seek refuge in Apulia. The county he gave to his own half-brother, Robert. He also expelled his kinsman William Busac, the second son of the count of Eu, and forced him into exile in France. The duke was not blood-thirsty in his dealings with his elder relatives, but he managed to rid himself of not a few.

The turning point in William's fortunes as duke was the death of his two greatest external enemies in 1060. Henry I's heir, Philip I, was a boy, to whom William's father-in-law, Baldwin of Flanders, was appointed guardian. William did homage to his overlord in 1060 at Dreux in the marches of Normandy and France, and, until Philip grew up, there was peace between them. The county of Anjou passed to a nephew of Geoffrey Martel, Geoffrey the Bearded, a weak ruler who soon had his brother, Fulk the Surly (*Rechinus*), as a rival. This was William's opportunity to carry out long-meditated plans against Maine, a conquest which William of Poitiers assures us was as much in accordance with the laws of justice as was the conquest of England. We are therefore given a diplomatic background which can usefully be compared with the English. Each reveals a patient accumulation of rights and claims in anticipation of the opportunity for military conquest.

To prepare the way William and his advisers built up the legend that the overlordship of Maine had been granted to the counts of Normandy by the king of France and that they had indeed possessed it at some time. In reality, at least since 1025, Angevin control over the county had been close and effective. As we have seen, William welcomed the exiled countess and her children, Herbert II and Margaret, in 1051. He accepted Herbert's homage and, as soon as he had children of his own, betrothed a daughter to Herbert and then his son and heir, Robert Curthose, to Margaret. He also obtained, we are told, an express concession from the young count that, should he die without issue, William was to be his heir, a bequest that he is said to have repeated on his death-bed. Thus until Herbert died in 1062 William could intervene in Maine on behalf of his vassal. After that William had a double claim—as Herbert's heir and as Margaret's guardian. Inevitably there were complications. When Herbert died another claimant intervened. This was Walter III, count of the Vexin, a nephew of King Edward the Confessor, who had married Biota of Maine, the dead count's aunt. Walter we notice was a possible pretender to the English throne. William had to face also the hostility, albeit ineffective, of Anjou and the disaffection of Geoffrey count of Mayenne who preferred the *status quo*. In 1063 William through wide devastations secured the surrender of Le Mans, the capital of Maine, and then, by setting fire to the town, the fortress of Mayenne. The intervener, Walter of Mantes, and his wife were captured and imprisoned at Falaise. Although it is not necessary to believe, as Orderic Vital alleged, that William had them poisoned, they certainly died in prison. As Margaret of Maine died about the time of the invasion, before her marriage to Robert Curthose could be canonically celebrated, the direct line of the comital family came to an end and William assumed the title of Count of Maine.

The possession of Maine and the quiescence of Anjou allowed William to turn against Brittany. He mounted a campaign, probably in 1064, which is illustrated on the Bayeux Tapestry because it comes into Harold's story, but which reveals the limitations to William's power. The young count, Conan II, William's kinsman, now out of tutelage, had refused to do homage to the duke, and was raiding the frontier. William led an army round and about Brittany, but finally withdrew both because of lack of provisions and because Geoffrey the Bearded, count of Anjou, moved to Conan's assistance. As a punitive raid it may have had some effect and the Bretons, especially through the sons of Eudo of Porhoët, contributed handsomely to William's expedition in 1066. But it was hardly a glorious campaign. Harold, who accompanied William, may easily have been contemptuous, especially since he himself had just campaigned in similar circumstances, and with far more success, against Wales.

By 1064, when William was thirty-seven, his reputation as a soldier and governor may have stood as high as Geoffrey of Anjou's a decade earlier and perhaps higher than, say, that of Theobald III of Blois, Chartres, and Champagne. But we may doubt whether he had the prestige of Baldwin of Flanders. He had risen while several of his seniors passed their peak and died. To his contemporaries he must have appeared as one who had arrived rather than as a coming man; and it was a dangerous as well as a competitive world.

Chapter Two

Military Society and the Art of War

WILLIAM and most of his vassals spent almost all their life, from boyhood until old age, engaged in war or in pursuits which were a training for war; and not a few, including the duke himself, found death on campaign. And so, in order to understand the careers, actions, and attitudes of these men we must study carefully the military organization and ideas of the time. As the chroniclers devote much of their space to wars this would appear to be an easy task, and unfortunately it has often been considered so. But in fact there are many difficulties. The chroniclers assume that their readers are familiar with typical detail; they rarely explain the composition of the armies or the tactics employed; and they wrote in Latin. Not only were they well versed in Caesar and other classical military writers and sometimes deliberately tried to give a Roman polish to eleventh-century commanders but they also had to use a vocabulary which was unsuited to their own times. For example, it is quite clear that they employed the word *miles*, which in classical Latin means an infantryman, and by the middle of the twelfth century, a knight, in several senses. Usually, however, it is the generic term for a soldier, irrespective of his service, rank, or social standing, just as we use the English word today.

The Norman chroniclers drew a distinction between, first, ducal forces casually assembled—the duke's own retinue reinforced by the contingents of friends and supporters; second, the ducal army for which summonses were sent out; and third, an army more widely recruited for a more serious campaign. The first type of army was essentially comprised of cavalry and of the most select kind. The duke and his barons rode with household retainers and enfeoffed knights, men of social standing who were familiar to them, indeed usually their friends and constant companions. These units formed the élite of any army.

The composition of the second category, the ducal army, is far less clear. We can assume that all William's barons, including most prelates, had to provide the duke with a contingent of soldiers; but whether these had to be cavalry, whether there was a fixed quota, and what were the length and conditions of service are obscure matters. There is some evidence that William took advantage of new enfeoffments and, in the church, new appointments to define more exactly the military service due from each vassal. But the quotas seem to have been small, a limitation of duty more in the interest of the vassal than of the duke. For larger contingents William seems to have looked outside his duchy. When Guy, count of Ponthieu, was captured at the battle of Mortemer in 1054 William kept him in prison at Bayeux for more than two years and only released him on condition that he became his vassal. Guy did homage and swore fealty and engaged to perform military service with a hundred soldiers each year wherever the duke should require it. Going farther afield, William paid the counts of Flanders a sum of money annually, known as a money-fief, and, if later conditions were in force, the count had to provide soldiers in return for this.

It is likely, therefore, that when William issued a summons to his army most of his vassals knew how many soldiers they had to bring with them; and we are probably safe in assuming that these would usually be cavalry. But there were probably exceptions. The contingents from Ponthieu and Flanders could have included infantry. And we notice that after the conquest of England, when the English army, or part of it, was brought over to Normandy under the kingdom's Norman barons, the contingents included native Englishmen who were possibly not trained to fight on horseback.

By the twelfth century the conditions of service in the royal and ducal armies were becoming minutely defined. It is unlikely, however, that there was much precision in William's army. There must have been customs; but the impression remains that the duke expected his barons and their forces to stay until the campaign was over or they were dismissed from it. When William, count of Arques, left the army without permission during the Domfront campaign of 1051–2, William was enraged.

As the size of an army composed of such duty forces cannot have been very large—probably to be counted in hundreds—the duke had to make other arrangements for any serious campaign. So had the individual baron if he were planning an important private war. There were first of all the military resources of the duchy itself beyond those tapped by the quotas, and then there were all the recruiting grounds outside the duchy : Brittany, Flanders, France, Auvergne, and Aquitaine. When William was committed to large-scale warfare, he often engaged Breton troops under their counts. It was also not unusual for William to recruit specialist troops, crossbowmen and engineers. The latter were mostly sappers, used to mine the walls of towns. William tried to undermine Exeter in 1068 and enfeoffed a few engineers in England. There is, however, no unambiguous evidence that William used siege engines of any kind, although their use was known to those who had had a classical education.

The mercenary troops were hired for a term, possibly forty days, at so much a day. They would expect a share of the booty—and we hear that William was generous in this respect—and, unless strictly controlled, were apt to set fire to a town in order to facilitate looting. They did not expect, however, to be rewarded with land. During the conquest of England William in desperation once offered his mutinous soldiers English fiefs if they would remain on protracted campaign. But all that they seem to have received was punishment. Nor did soldiers expect to be consulted. When William asked his troops whether he should accept the proffered English crown they were astonished at his action. We can believe that they were mostly ruffians, attracted to the career through a variety of circumstances, mainly unfortunate, and for a variety of reasons, largely dishonourable.

Military equipment is beautifully shown on the Bayeux Tapestry. A cavalryman wore a mailed shirt, the *byrnie*

(Old-English) or *hauberk* (French), made of inter-linked iron rings, which covered his body, upper arms and thighs, and, when there was a coif, his neck and, if he chose, his head. Sometimes he wore gaiters of mail on his legs. But he had no protective covering for his wrists, hands, or feet. On his head he wore a conical iron helmet with a bar-like extension, a nasal, to protect the upper part of his face from slashes. The horses had no trappers or armour. The rider, however, carried a kite-shaped shield, rounded at the top, made of leather stretched over a wooden frame, and this gave his left side some protection. Since armour of iron plate was at least as easy to make as mail (and the technique was actually employed with the helmet), we cannot doubt that the defensive equipment of the period was designed for swift raids and skirmishes and that complete protection was deliberately sacrificed for speed and movement. The hauberk probably weighed under 20lb and was little burden to a horseman in the saddle. Duke William, while operating from Hastings before the battle, once returned on foot owing to the difficulty of the path and not only wore or carried his own hauberk but shouldered William fitzOsbern's as well. Moreover, except against the heaviest weapons, such as the battle-axe, the armour gave adequate protection. Arrows and spears could not penetrate the mail and rarely pierced the shield. The risk of serious bruising was, of course, considerable.

But far more vulnerable than the rider was his mount. And since the stallions ridden in battle were expensive and highly prized, the lack of protection given to them proves that it was unusual to fight on horse against infantry or against prepared positions which could be strengthened with sharpened stakes and other obstacles to horses. The offensive weapons of the cavalryman were a long straight sword used for slashing and a lance or spear for stabbing and more often for throwing as a javelin. Some carried, instead of the lance, a cudgel, a useful weapon in a mêlée. All probably had a knife or dagger. The commanders flew flags, *gonfanons*, from their spears. The shields too carried designs. At Dinant in 1064 the duke had a floral cross and stars on his shield. Dragons and geometrical patterns were popular. But neither the flags nor the shields were truly heraldic—they did not bear devices peculiar to the man and his family. It was always necessary when a man wished to identify himself to describe what armour and shield he would wear on that particular day. William probably had many shields, each differently adorned.

The Bayeux Tapestry probably gives an ideal picture of the troops' equipment. Their discipline and skill can also be exaggerated. It is unlikely that hired cavalry was always thoroughly trained or had been drilled in long-standing units. Sometimes auxiliaries and mercenaries were engaged in bands under a leader; but there are many references to soldiers, individually or with a few companions, seeking their fortune in the wars. Nor were the troops rigidly specialized. These armies, although they rode on the march, did not always fight mounted. As cavalry were presumably paid higher wages than infantry, for they had to maintain their mounts, it was certainly uneconomical to use them as foot. But when military necessity demanded they were probably not deterred by knightly pride from dismounting. Horses, after all, were expensive, and no cavalry soldier would have wished to risk his charger when conditions were unsuitable.

The military strategy of the period was based almost entirely on the castle or town. To capture the fortresses of the enemy and to maintain one's own was the basic intention of every commander. The castles, whether of simple *motte* and *bailey* construction, such as are shown on the Bayeux Tapestry, or stone fortifications reinforced by natural features—hills, rocks, and rivers—did not deny the country to an invader. He could pass between them and move freely over the open countryside, but he advanced at the risk of sorties from the castles, surprise attacks on his rear, and ambushes laid for him. And his object could be no more than the devastation of the countryside and the seizure of booty. Many campaigns were indeed limited to this purpose and were nothing but punitive raids. If, however, the object was to conquer territory then the castles and towns had to be taken, and the garrisons replaced.

The motte and bailey castle was at its simplest a mound of earth (the motte) formed by the excavation of a circular ditch, in method of construction similar to a child's sand castle. The motte was surmounted by a wooden palisade and a wooden keep, to which ladders gave access. Adjacent to the motte was a bailey, an area defended by a ditch and rampart and possibly a palisade, within which were the living quarters and workshops of the garrison. The bailey was abandoned for the motte in the last resort. Probably most important barons had at least one castle more elaborate than this and often sited within a fortified, or at least defensible, place, making it necessary for the attacker first to get possession of the town.

The warfare of the period was so indecisive because the defence had the advantage over the attack. William, with no siege engines and few engineers, was never able to take a town or reputable castle by assault. He had to employ rudimentary tactics. He aimed first at entering a castle or town by surprise, hoping to catch the garrison or burgesses unaware and burst in before the drawbridge was up or the gates shut. If this failed threats or bribery were tried. There was always the implicit threat of loot. A town which did not surrender on terms was usually put to the sack. But it was unusual to massacre the inhabitants or soldiers. When William took Mayenne in 1063 the victors found a rich booty—noble horses, arms and armour, and all kinds of furnishing. This, like the booty taken elsewhere in the campaign, William, 'because he was a most self-controlled and liberal prince', allotted to the army rather than to himself. There was also the devastation of the countryside, which not only denied food to the besieged but reminded them of a nearer fate. Savagery was rare. But in 1051-2, when William showed his ferocity before Alençon, two towns with their castles surrendered to him. Bribery was more merciful and sometimes succeeded; but on the whole the loyalty of garrisons to their lord is characteristic of the period. To set fire to the buildings was often possible for there were always wooden structures in towns and castles. William fired the town of Alençon in 1051-2, Mayenne in 1063, and the castle of Dinant in 1064 (shown on the Bayeux Tapestry). But arson, like cruelty, was probably considered reprehensible and had to be justified before public opinion by special circumstances. When these various methods had been tried and failed, or had been rejected, only a blockade remained. Usually, as we see from Domfront in 1051–2 and Arques in 1053, one or more simple castles were thrown up by the attackers in order to protect the blockading force, and then the main army could pass on or disperse. This method was cheap in cost of life and manpower, for a besieging party scarcely larger than the garrison was required.

Poitiers' account of William's reduction of Le Mans in 1063 illustrates many of these points. He writes :

> He had the skill and force available to set fire to it immediately, destroy the whole town, and massacre the guilty. But with his usual restraint he preferred to spare men's blood, however culpable, and leave unharmed this strongly fortified city, the capital fortress of the land he had conquered. He therefore chose this way of subduing it—to sow terror by frequent attacks and long sojourns in its neighbourhood, to devastate its vineyards, fields, and demesnes, to capture all the castles round about, to set up garrisons wherever advisable, and finally to inflict without respite all possible hardships.

These tactics were successful and Le Mans surrendered. For political reasons no punishment was inflicted; but the surrender of the castle was required. Walter of Mantes, yielding to threats, gave his permission, and the whole city passed into William's hands. The duke then had new fortifications constructed within the walls in order to overawe the citizens.

Because of the nature of the campaigns fighting was associated mainly with the blockade and relief of castles, and was largely of the skirmish type. Both beleaguered and beleaguers, the relieving and the covering forces, had plenty of leisure for devising ruses and tactical schemes which kept them happy without great danger. But larger battles were also fought, as Val-des-dunes (1047) and Mortemer (1054), when it was essential to prevent large rebel or invading forces from roaming at will. To secure a pitched battle it was usually necessary to send a challenge and for it to be accepted. And there were customs which were often observed. Before William invaded Maine, probably in 1054, he sent Geoffrey Martel of Anjou a formal defiance, giving forty days' notice that for certain reasons he was going to build a castle at Ambrières. The reasons presumably were his claim to the county. In 1051–2, when Geoffrey rode to relieve Domfront, he informed William's scouts that he would reach the town at dawn on the following day and he described the horse he would be riding and his dress and shield. William described his accoutrement in return. Neither of these challenges, it may be remarked, led in fact to a battle. Conan II of Brittany usually announced on what day he would attack the Norman frontier. The formal defiance of the enemy seems to have been regarded by all feudal society as proper gentlemanly conduct.

Battles differed little from skirmishes except in size. Problems of command hardly arose after the first dispositions had been made, for the feudal components were uncontrollable. What was required of a commander was personal bravery and example and the ability to intervene, especially to give succour, if the opportunity emerged. Although to command in a set battle probably called for no special qualities or training it should be noticed that William was without this experience in 1066. He had been present at Val-des-dunes and had cut up Henry's rear at Varaville. But he had never deployed his own army in the face of a large enemy force.

The usual tactics were to get the cavalry, which was in squadrons under their feudal lords and captains, strung out in a line, and then send it against the enemy. The supreme commander often remained in the rear with a select reserve. Spears were thrown as the distance closed and then it was hand-to-hand fighting with lances, swords, or cudgels. The side with the greater weight, coherence, and determination forced the other to break off and turn tail. An unco-ordinated pursuit followed. This was the most dangerous part of the action. Riders could be thrown and limbs broken. As river crossings were few, horsemen could be driven into the water or destroyed at congested bridges. And as, except in the largest engagements, there was rarely infantry to slaughter, battles were still lethal for knights. Not a few important men lost their lives in this Norman warfare.

William, his barons, and their knights spent all their days in the open air on horseback. When they were not fighting they were on the move and hunted as they went. Their strategic conceptions can be considered rudimentary, even their grasp of battle tactics was slender, but in the art of small-scale fighting they had nothing to learn, and they were probably well qualified by character to command mercenaries and auxiliaries. These virtues and limitations of the military forces available to William must be remembered when his invasion of England and subsequent campaigns are discussed.

Chapter Three

The Duke's Government and the Ducal Church

A FEUDAL prince ruled in person. He could not do without many servants—companions and advisers, a military escort, priests and chaplains, the personal servants of his household, and the officials on his estates—but he was not hidden behind the formalities of a court or the impediments of a bureaucracy. He lived in rustic state in the public view; he was always on the move; and he was accessible. He was expected to do justice in person to men and women both great and small, and if he was wise all the threads of his government were gathered into his own hands. Indeed, feudal rule began to decay once direct personal relations between the lord and his vassals and, more tenuously, with all his people, became impossible.

Normandy is about the size of south-eastern England, say the shires of Kent, Sussex, Surrey, and Hampshire, with Berkshire thrown in for good measure. It could all be kept under the duke's vigilant eye and its rule did not require an elaborate machinery. Orders could be sent by the mouth of messengers. The memory of grants of lands and privileges and of duties could be kept in the head. And it is not in the least surprising that we know little of the details of ducal administration before 1066 : there was probably little worth the mention. It has sometimes been called a centralized government. This is a misleading description. Ducal government was in the hands of the duke, and William pressed hard on his vassals because he was a vigorous man and Normandy was small. To suggest, however, that there was an omnicompetent central government which touched everybody is quite absurd.

Primarily William only ruled his own demesne—his barons, his bishops and monasteries, his household, and his private estates. His barons, bishops, and abbots ruled their demesnes similarly. Like all feudal societies it was essentially a decentralized organization, a hierarchical system with each feudal lord little concerned except with the rung beneath him, his own servants and vassals.

William's barons attended his court, especially at the great church festivals and when there was some important business to discuss. Complaints of the duke against a baron or disputes between the barons themselves would properly be heard there. Business which needed common consent because it depended on the co-operation of the barons—such as the making of war—must have been discussed. We know that Duke Robert secured assent to his nomination of William as his heir, and it is likely that William proposed the invasion of England at a meeting with his barons. But the social aspect of feudal courts was still dominant in this period. Vassals expected to be feasted by their lord, to have an opportunity to talk with him, to ask for favours, to denounce rivals, to impress their point of view. Conversely the lord wished to see his barons, keep an eye on them, do them justice, and ensure that they were content. We do not in fact read much of William's courts before 1066. He seems to have been parsimonious with his own goods, and, except for the rejoicings in 1067, eschewed splendour and conviviality. Even if he was not grim, he was hardly open-handed.

William's greatest governmental achievement was gradually to enforce law and order in the duchy, and this was not done administratively. The most important barons, those who shared with the prince the title of count, were originally close kinsmen of the ruling family. And, owing to the promiscuousness of the early counts, there were few barons who could not claim the honour of some relationship. William, as we have seen, suffered much trouble from the ambitions and independence of his kinsmen. But the fertility of the dukes had been diminishing and once William's older kinsmen had been ruined or had died there were few left who were really closely related to him. He himself had merely two half-brothers to endow; one received the bishopric of Bayeux and the other the county of Mortain. Thus the class of baron who had a blood-right to independence almost disappeared and there remained an inter-related community, often quarrelling but basically in harmony, which recognized the duke as its head. The duke was not only the lord of the land and the lord of vassals, he was also head of the family. All the recent dukes had tried to control private baronial wars, both by personal intervention and by encouraging the Truce of God. They took the line that quarrels between barons should be heard in the ducal court and not decided by war. Only the strongest of them, however, had much success. The Truce of God, an ecclesiastical measure to prohibit warfare at certain times and seasons, was welcomed by William and, significantly, was first promulgated by a church council immediately after the battle of Val-des-dunes (1047), and by most Norman councils thereafter. William transformed God's truce almost into a ducal peace.

William in the end secured a firmer internal peace than had ever been experienced before in the duchy. He tried to disregard some of the complications of a vassal having several lords and seems to have insisted, when he could, that his barons owed their loyalty to him alone. For example, when a Norman army under Robert count of Eu and Roger of Mortemer defeated the French army at Mortemer-sur-Eaulne in 1054, Count Ralf of Montdidier could have been captured had not Roger helped him. Roger had done Ralf homage in the past, presumably for some land he held of him, and so he hid him in his castle for three days and then conducted him home. Roger, by refusing to capture his lord, probably behaved honourably by the standards of the time. But the duke viewed his conduct otherwise and banished him from the county. Later he gave Roger back his fief; but the *caput* of the honour, the castle of Mortemer, he withheld and granted it to William of Warenne, Roger's kinsman, a true vassal. William of Warenne, or his son of the same name, was given the honour of Lewes in England and was created, probably by William Rufus, earl of Surrey. The Mortimers established themselves in England under William fitz-

Osbern, lord of Breteuil and earl of Hereford, and did not become earls until the fourteenth century.

William also struck at the military independence of his vassals by controlling their fortifications. He destroyed new and unlicensed baronial castles after each rebellion and, if we can believe Orderic's dramatic story of the reaction of some barons to the news of William's death, the duke had developed the practice of putting ducal garrisons into baronial castles at least in a military emergency and into those of his vassals whom he did not trust. This ducal right became the custom in both Normandy and England, and was resented. From the later history of both countries we can see how much a baron prized castles as a symbol of his rank and how slighted he felt when deprived of them. William may also have begun to make the feudal services of his vassals more precise—a policy which could have suited both parties—and, as we would expect, William tried to discipline the armies he commanded. William of Poitiers at two points in his story wrote, 'The herds and flocks of the farmers grazed safely on the fields and wastes. The corn was not trampled by the proud hooves of the cavalry or cut by the forager, but remained intact for the reaper's sickle. The weak and unarmed rode singing on their horse where they chose without trembling at the sight of squadrons of knights.' William's armies were indeed probably dissuaded from the worst excesses by ducal edicts; but, as we shall see from their conduct between 1066 and 1070 in England, Poitiers paints an idealized picture.

In Normandy, unlike England, there was no written law in the eleventh century. But we can assume, on the evidence of later compilations, that the law was a variety of Germanic law—putting a value on each man according to his rank—modified by feudal customs. The duke by his office was the greatest avenger of the law and he had a high jurisdiction (the pleas of the sword) over offences against public order. The capital crimes most often mentioned are murder, arson, and robbery. But the duke also claimed responsibility for the peace of the cultivators and of travellers on the high roads and for the protection of widows and orphans. William, we are told by his admirers, hated to destroy what God had created and, in his mercy, substituted mutilation of limbs for the death penalty. We know that he mutilated, and the only man he is known to have executed is Earl Waltheof in 1076, a strange exception. The duke had no monopoly of jurisdiction, not even perhaps of the highest; and the barons and churches with judicial rights would not have recognized that they had delegated powers, although they might grudgingly have allowed that the duke had overriding control.

Little is known except in outline of the ducal household and ducal administration either of justice or of finance. The household seems to have been modelled on the Capetian-Carolingian court and differed little from the English except in nomenclature. William's most important household servant was his steward, Osbern, and then his son, William fitzOsbern, whom the duke was to reward magnificently in England. Other servants were the chamberlain and butler and possibly a constable. The chamberlain was in charge of the bedchamber (*camera ducis*), which, as in England, was probably the household treasury. There were priests and clerks, chaplains, at court, but, like the English and unlike the French, there was no chancellor. The duke, however, differed from the English king in having no seal for authenticating documents and no identifiable secretariat. His household neither issued documents nor kept archives.

In the duchy at large the duke's most important officials were his *vicomtes*. The office had become hereditary and was held by important barons and it was a great achievement for William to have brought the *vicomtes* into real subjection and even perhaps increased the number of *vicomtés*. As after the Conquest the English shire-reeves were renamed *vicomtes* the office must have been similar : a multi-competent administrative post but with the weight on the financial, judicial, and military duties. The *vicomtes*, like the sheriffs, 'farmed' the profits of their office, that is to say they did not account for the ducal revenues they collected but paid a fixed agreed rent. They also acted under commission as ducal judges and had military responsibilities, especially in defence, often acting as custodians of ducal castles. William possibly had more rights, financial and judicial, than most counts in France and, more important, he gradually enforced them. The re-establishment of his rights after his minority and the anarchy gave him experience which was to be useful when he became king of England.

Normandy was still ruled by custom and oral tradition. A society largely without records and written documents is indeed primitive in that respect but should not be re-garded as backward. William for his scale of government simply did not need much apparatus. When, however, he became king of England he took over a more sophisticated and literary administration without any difficulty. Nor should the rule of custom be interpreted as a sign of a stagnant society. Codes of law, written custumals, manuals of procedure, and such like, could have a petrifying effect. Unwritten custom was remarkably plastic and it is obvious that Normandy changed enormously in the century-and-a-half after its foundation.

There was, of course, one literate body in Normandy, the church; and it is in the ecclesiastical setting that Wil-liam assumes some of the appearance of a civilized ruler, indeed almost the position of a king. By keeping himself at the head of the church William had the opportunity to make himself better acquainted with more advanced governmental techniques, for the church had begun to produce written documents, to legislate in council, and to develop an administration. He also entered a world influ-enced by ideas, even rent by intellectual controversy, and although he acquired no taste for speculation, his fami-liarity with ecclesiastical institutions and his ease with ecclesiastical persons, together with his simple piety, were always an advantage to him. The church repaid William for his benevolent protection by supporting his policies, by giving a moral justification for a few of his more doubt-ful actions, and by supplying him with some skilled and faithful servants.

The tone of the Norman church changed considerably during William's rule. The primary cause was the infiltra-tion of various religious movements which had arisen else-where in Christendom, such as the more austere view of the monastic life, the renewed interest in theology, the attempt to enforce uncorrupted ecclesiastical law, and the demand for more and better education. There was also the introduction of new styles of church architecture. William was not an initiator in any of these matters, but, because he was a God-fearing man, he welcomed them to the best of his understanding. This was the accepted role of the lay patron : what the church required was protection, encouragement, and generosity from the lay powers. And, because William protected and encouraged, Normandy was visited by some exceptional men, who would have been differently received in other counties and kingdoms. Germans were made abbots of Rouen (Holy Trinity), St. Pierre-sur-Dive, and St. Wandrille, and an Angevin abbot of Grestain. Italians and Burgundians gave even more lustre.

It was, however, the inner tone rather than the outward appearance which changed more in this period. Members of the ducal family held the archbishopric of Rouen from 987 until 1087, except for 1055–67, and the bishoprics of Bayeux from 1015 to 1099, Lisieux from 1049 to 1077, and Avranches from 1060 to 1067. And if William appointed the foreign monk, Maurilius, to Rouen in 1055 he also put his half-brother, Odo, into Bayeux in 1049 when yet a youth. These bishops were not saints; few were even respectable in morals; but they had a high regard for their dignity and rights, they were mostly builders, often organizers, and were generally adequately educated. John, bishop of Avranches 1060–7, and then archbishop of Rouen, 1067–87, even wrote a book on the liturgy.

The kinship between the duke and some of the bishops, although not without inconveniences, at least encouraged the formation of an ecclesiastical pyramid corresponding to the secular hierarchy; and on the whole the bishops were more obedient than the counts to their duke. Although secular magnates, with feudal vassals and sometimes many knights, they tended to look to the duke for protection against their neighbours. They also encouraged him to preside over their councils so as to commit him to their policies. The councils or synods held by the arch-

bishops of Rouen from about 1042, and attended by the
bishops and abbots, prove that the prelates were trying to
govern. Archbishop Mauger's council of *c.* 1042 contained
some criticism of his nephew the duke's behaviour, and
his unrestrained attack on all aspects of simony (the selling of ecclesiastical offices and sacraments) was probably
intended to injure William. But Archbishop Maurilius'
councils at Rouen in 1063 and at Lisieux in 1064, at which
the principal target was the unchastity and marriage of
priests, were fully to William's taste and received his
full support. Other abuses were attacked by these councils; and we see that the main purpose was to improve the
conduct of the lower clergy. These were the first shots in a
campaign; the main offensive was mounted after 1067
when John of Avranches became metropolitan; but it is
clear that the Norman prelates were becoming increasingly receptive to some aspects of the reform movement
which was developing in Christendom, and that the
Norman church, even if generally lax, was certainly not
complacent at the top.

Legislation in synods would have been useless had not
the bishops possessed officials and ecclesiastical courts to
enforce the decrees. The bishop's principal judicial officers
were his archdeacons who sometimes were enfeoffed with
their office. The bishop and his archdeacons held courts
in which ran the law of the church, canon law. According
to Norman custom the bishop and his servants had the
exclusive right to conduct the various ordeals by which
most types of legal disputes could be settled, and the
bishop was also allowed a jurisdiction which can be
divided into three competences : jurisdiction over sacred
places and their inhabitants, the right to punish criminous
or offending members of the clergy, and the similar, but
far more restricted, right to punish the sinful laity (including jurisdiction in matrimonial suits). But all this
ecclesiastical jurisdiction was regarded concretely as the
rights of a bishop—*leges episcopales*—not ideologically as
a division between God and Caesar determined by the
application of a principle, and the duke treated it like
any other franchisal jurisdiction, controlling, limiting, or
extending it as he thought wise or fit. In 1080 at Lille-

bonne he regulated it drastically with little regard to principle. At the same time he always encouraged episcopal jurisdiction when he approved the purpose. He lent it every support when it was directed to the repression of crime and vice, especially among the clergy. He even punished ecclesiastical judges when they were remiss. But he had not the slightest intention of allowing encroachment by the church on his own rights, or on those of his barons. Do your duty, and do it better, and keep to your proper duties, was his attitude.

William is said by Poitiers to have been regular in attendance at mass, attentive to the precepts of the clergy, and particularly favourable to monks. The anonymous writer, perhaps a monk of Caen, who describes William's death, simply copied out a few phrases from Chapter 26 of Einhard's *Life of Charles the Great* to portray William as a church-goer. This plagiarism is not serious. All these writers were idealizing an attitude common among soldiers. The knight, because of his dangerous profession, was often a petitioner for divine aid and protection, yet he usually despised priests both because of their calling and because of their 'hypocrisy' : they were men who reproved vice in others while living a sinful life themselves. Unlike a loyal vassal they were not 'straight'. Monks, however, escaped this contempt. They were the *militia Christi*, the soldiers of God, and it was obvious to all that they struggled manfully and loyally to serve their lord. By William's time, therefore, the barons were outstripping the duke in the foundation of monasteries, in which they hoped to place holy monks who would intercede with God for the founder and his family and pray for his safety and success. At the Battle of Hastings were two bishops, Odo of Bayeux and Geoffrey of Coutances, and many clerks and monks. They were there, Poitiers reminds us, to fight with prayers. With shrewd justice and proper gratitude William robbed the English church after his victory in order to reward those Norman monasteries which had laboured in his cause. The Breton houses, possibly because of the rout at Hastings, were significantly overlooked.

William himself made small voluntary addition to the nine abbeys and one nunnery which he inherited from his father. He built in Normandy the two houses at Caen as a penance for his incestuous marriage and an abbey at Montebourg and, in England, Battle to atone for the slaughter at Hastings. The fashion had, however, spread to the magnates, and his barons and knights founded some seventeen monasteries and six nunneries in the duchy, sometimes restoring to the church land which earlier had been taken from the older monasteries. It will be noticed that the duke was not prodigal with his own inherited revenues. Indeed most of his foundations were made on the cheap. When he came to be buried in St Stephen's, Caen, Ascelin fitzArthur claimed that the duke had unjustly despoiled his father of the land on which the church was built. Whether the charge was true or false—and Ascelin had his supporters present—there must have been some arbitrariness in the transaction, and Ascelin was bought off so that the ceremony could proceed. Nor did Battle cost William much. It was, however, counted to his piety that he allowed his barons to devote their resources to the foundation of monasteries, and confirmed all their charters, for, from a narrowly military standpoint, it was a wastage of resources.

Poitiers believed that in William's time Normandy rivalled with its monasteries the Egypt of old. The internal condition of these Norman convents is far from clear owing to the paucity of evidence. Later Norman opinion seems to have been that the monasteries were in a poor condition in 1035 and that during William's principality there was remarkable progress in all directions. There was a strong medical and teaching tradition going back to William of Dijon, and certainly by 1066 the convents were producing monks whose literary works or reputation were to be remembered : for example, William *Calculus*, monk of Jumièges, who soon after 1070 wrote his thin and muddled history of the Norman dukes, and Durand, monk of St Wandrille, a pupil of the German Isembert, and later abbot of Troarn, who composed in rather elegant Latin a theological treatise against Berengar of Tours. The great ultramontanes, John of Ravenna, Lanfranc of Pavia, and Anselm of Aosta, were at Fécamp, Caen, and Bec respectively. Yet Lanfranc's high reputation in the duchy is proof that the scholastic standard was relatively low, and one of the most skilful writers, William of Poitiers, was not a monk but a secular clerk and archdeacon who had been educated in the city after which he was named. In general it appears that the older houses were improving their literary and artistic culture and that the new ones were only just beginning to find time for it. Piety, not learning, was still the dominant ideal. The abbey of Bec is a famous example of a poor foundation, remarkable at first only for the simple unlettered piety of the community, which grew into a great home of learning and became an ornament not only to Normandy but to Western Christendom at large.

We know something about the early history of Bec because one of its monks, Gilbert Crispin, who became abbot of Westminster, wrote tenderly about its founder, Herlwin, and the other great architect of its fortunes, Lanfranc, both his masters. Herlwin, nobly born and a knight of Gilbert, count of Brionne, Duke William's uncle, renounced the world in his prime for reasons which are not perfectly clear. Once he had obtained his lord's permission he gave his hereditary estates to the church and about 1034, just before Duke Robert left for Jerusalem, built with his own hands a chapel on his lands at Bonneville. At night he learned to read the psalter. He visited neighbouring monasteries in order to learn the Rule, and, despite his disappointment with them, razed his old home at Bonneville and built in its place a house for monks. Herbert, bishop of Lisieux (1026–50), consecrated the church, accepted the monastic professions of Herlwin and of two of his retainers, later conferred priests' orders on Herlwin, and, when the community grew, made him abbot. At Bonneville the monks lived like peasants, cultivating the land; and even the recruitment of Herlwin's mother to wash and cook for them only emphasizes the stark misery of their physical life. The place Herlwin had chosen was remote and barren and two miles from the nearest spring. It was decided to move to another of Herlwin's estates, at Bec, on a stream from which it took its name, in one of the wooded valleys near Brionne. A wooden church and cloister were built, but the monastic range collapsed; the place was insalubrious; and soon there was murmuring among the monks and some desertion. About 1042, as though sent by God, Lanfranc of Pavia stopped there and was converted. He too almost ran away, a scholar disgusted by the coarseness of life and the brutality of the monks; but he stayed and after three years began to teach again.

Lanfranc's fame as a scholar brought modest wealth to the abbey and also the problem of space. He became prior and ruled the monks while Herlwin was busy with the estates. Soon Lanfranc was urging a short move to a better and larger site. In 1060 Anselm of Aosta and a few companions entered the monastery and within a short time Herlwin's reluctance to move again was overcome and the new buildings were started. Lanfranc left in 1063 to be abbot of Caen and then archbishop of Canterbury. But he returned in his splendour as 'primate of All Britain' in October 1077 to dedicate the new church. Bec had become rich in estates, populous, and famous. The crowds at the dedication were so great and enthusiastic that many of the monks were crowded out of their own ceremonies. But the king and queen, although in Normandy, were not there. Bec was, perhaps, something that William did not fully understand. Herlwin barely survived his proudest day, dying in 1078 at the age of eight-four, and Anselm succeeded him as abbot. In the forty-four years of Herlwin's rule a complete transformation had taken place; yet it was the knight who had learned to read only in middle age who was loved and respected above all others by the monks.

Gilbert Crispin remembered Herlwin and Lanfranc with almost equal respect and affection, and it is a testimonial to the tone at Bec that he could worship two masters placed poles apart in their religion. It was Lanfranc who gave Bec the stamp which was to bring it later fame. A Lombard from Pavia, restless in his youth and avid for learning, he studied in Italian schools and then, a wandering scholar, found his way to Normandy where he set up his own school at Avranches. He was hailed as the greatest master of the liberal arts in Europe, and was especially esteemed as a dialectician, an exponent of the

art of argument. But once he entered religion he renounced worldly learning, for he now regarded the pagan
authors as unseemly, faith and doctrine as outside the
scope of dialectical exercises, and rhetoric as unsuited to
a monk. He turned to the two basic monastic studies, the
Bible and canon law. He made no lasting reputation in
either field. Since—both of necessity and by choice—
when expounding the Scriptures he confined himself to
the elucidation of meaning, his commentaries were soon
thought elementary and dull. His collection of canon law
and his rule for his Canterbury monks became influential
in England after the Conquest and he was often consulted
by friends and colleagues on legal, liturgical, and doctrinal
points. But his works and opinions were quickly out-
moded. Lanfranc introduced a flurry of theological
interest into Normandy when he turned against one of his
masters, Berengar of Tours, and championed conservative
doctrine against the more speculative and, it was alleged,
heretical views of the dialectical school on the mystery of
the Eucharist. Normandy took pride in its champion, all
the more since Berengar was protected by Anjou; and
William showed his orthodoxy by persecuting Berengar's
followers. Yet Lanfranc's real achievement was not in the
realm of creative thought but as a schoolmaster. To earn
money for Bec he founded a school which attracted pupils,
some to become more distinguished than himself. And as
William's spiritual adviser he was able to influence ecclesiastical affairs.

Lanfranc, although he became abbot of Caen in 1063
and archbishop of Canterbury in 1070, having refused
Rouen in 1067, was not a careerist but a man seeking a
way. His worldly success was largely due to his catching
one tide after another and being borne along. He emerged
as a man perfectly fitted to advise a prince well-disposed
towards the church. Always he had sought authority, and
he was ever happiest as a second-in-command. Except for
his one sharp disagreement with his duke—apparently
over William's marriage—he never came into conflict
with the lay power and, indeed, served William faithfully
in many secular tasks. He also had a great respect for the
reformed papacy and much sympathy with its aims. As

a monk he was an ardent opponent of clerical marriage and all sexual depravity. It is unlikely that he gave any thought to the political consequences of some of the ideas being advocated in the papal *curia*, and whenever there was a conflict of law or policy he sheltered behind his duke and king. Lanfranc and William could work happily and fruitfully together.

William was always the master. He stood no nonsense from his abbots and monks. Just as he secured the deposition of his uncle, Mauger, archbishop of Rouen, so in 1061 he drove out another kinsman, Robert of Grandmesnil, abbot of St Évroult, for unwise words during a rebellion involving the abbot's family. According to Orderic Vital, Robert went to Rome, and when he returned with papal legates and letters of restitution and confronted the duke at Lillebonne, William exclaimed that he would receive with reverence the nuncios of the pope in any matter of faith and religion, but if any monk from his land brought a false accusation against him he would irreverently hang him from the highest oak in the nearby wood. The story may be apocryphal, but William, despite considerable pressure from many sides, steadfastly refused to allow Robert back. As usual his motives were mixed. He removed an abbot who was a kinsman of the founder and appointed a good and artistic man, Osbern, in his place. But he was also punishing a rebellious family. And William could be ferocious. When Lanfranc opposed him, perhaps over his marriage, he ordered him out of the country and ducal servants to burn down one of the monastery's villages. Lanfranc was pardoned but the village had been destroyed.

William's attitude to the papacy was of a piece with his views on the proper place of religion. There is no reason to doubt that, especially under the influence of Lanfranc, he held the successor to St Peter in due honour, as a spiritual prince who possessed certain important spiritual powers, more, as his father in God. He accepted that the pope was the final arbiter in matters of faith and was reminded of it by the current dispute over the orthodoxy of Berengar's doctrines. He knew that the pope claimed a special responsibility for the morals of princes, for his own incestuous marriage had been banned. He was aware that the pope could deny his services since Archbishop Mauger of Rouen had failed to obtain the pallium. He could see that recent popes had become more active in reform because the Norman church had been summoned to Leo IX's council at Rheims in 1049 and had been well represented. From his acquaintance with the affairs of the Normans in Italy and Sicily he learned that the pope could be an ally or an enemy, could even lead an army—and be captured. In other words, the pope had rights and claims, like any other ruler, and these were sometimes acceptable, sometimes inadmissible. They were there for the duke to invoke when it was convenient to do so. William obtained papal legates in 1054-5 in order to give proper form to his own deposition of Archbishop Mauger, and in 1067 secured papal consent to his intention to transfer Bishop John from Avranches to Rouen. In 1066 he put his case against King Harold to the papal court. On the other hand these powers were to be circumvented when applied uninvited or inconveniently. William married Matilda despite the papal ban and refused to dismiss her, but he was willing to do penance in 1059 when Lanfranc had negotiated an acceptable peace. He refused to allow the pope to interfere in any way with his patronage over the Norman church. They were his bishoprics and especially they were his monasteries. William was ready to withstand any action which he believed infringed his own rights. His attitude to the pope was basically no different from his relationship with his feudal overlord, the king of France.

Chapter Four

The English Scene

THE Normans were fully aware of England. The same Vikings had raided both England and Neustria in the ninth and tenth centuries, and it was a matter of chance on which side of the Channel they settled. The Danelaw was the English Normandy. Yet from that time the two countries had begun to draw steadily apart. England, under Svein Forkbeard, his son, Cnut, and his grandsons, became more Scandinavian in tone during the very period when the Normans were adopting French customs. In 1066 an English king, with the Danish name of Haraldr, faced a Norman duke with the French name, Guillelme. Memory of kinship between the two nations was probably falling into oblivion. But the remembrance of English plunder had not been lost. If some Normans chose to make their fortunes in Apulia, others knew that there was much richer booty, even if more carefully guarded, closer to their shores.

England was one of the wealthiest countries in western Europe. A good climate for agriculture and husbandry and rich mineral resources, easy access to the sea and excellent ports, had produced a precocious urban development which fed on, and itself encouraged, trade. The silver coin, let alone the treasures, which the Vikings had extorted from England at the turn of the tenth century, was a marvel throughout Europe. In more peaceful days, especially under Edward the Confessor, the English royal court attracted fortune-hunters, both lay and clerical, from all Christian lands. Among these were Normans. With Robert, abbot of Jumièges, as bishop of London and merchants of Rouen trading busily with that city, we may be sure that the rewards which England had to offer were well known in the duchy.

Moreover, by 1052 England was ruled by an ageing and childless king who had no obvious heir. Here indeed was a chance for an adventurer! Edward, even when stripped of the ecclesiastical legend created for him in the twelfth century, remains an enigmatic figure. The son of the English Æthelred and the Norman Emma, reared in England during Viking invasions, then forced to take asylum in Normandy and the neighbouring lands, he came late and untrained into his royal inheritance. His reign, lying between those of the Danish Harthacnut and the Anglo-Danish Harold, was a sort of quiet parenthesis in English history; and, as it recaptured something of the Old-English past, became regarded later as a golden age. That he was a successful king cannot be doubted. He over-came vigorously all his initial difficulties, solved adroitly most of those which arose later, and gave his country twenty-three tranquil years. By most early writers Edward was likened to Solomon, which signifies 'peace'.

Yet it is doubtful whether Edward was in fact a man of peace. He came of martial stock; he was always prepared to fight; and he hunted indefatigably. Although he often chose the easiest way out of his difficulties, and usually, in internal politics, preferred to play one interest against another in order to get his own way, he was ruthless to enemies when there was no hindrance. In his early years as king he exiled several leaders of the Scandinavian party. In 1051 he banished his father-in-law, Earl Godwin of Wessex, and temporarily broke the whole family. He was still banishing men in 1065. A contemporary describes him as a man terrible in his anger, like a lion.

After 1052, however, Edward was in decline. Years of patient intrigue, interspersed with bouts of violence, were replaced by a period in which he relied increasingly for government and action on the children of Earl Godwin, especially on Queen Edith, Harold, earl of Wessex, and Tostig, earl of Northumbria. The queen ruled the court and the earls the two main frontiers. This arrangement gave the monarchy formidable power. The other earls were young and there was no party in the country which could threaten the government, provided it remained united. The rebellion in 1065, which drove Tostig out of

Northumbria, was only successful because Harold refused to suppress it, indeed was possibly its instigator.

The one weakness in the political situation was the lack of an heir to the throne. There is no good evidence that Edward had taken a vow of chastity as a youth, and there are many reasons for doubting it. But he does not seem to have been much interested in women and was still unmarried when, in his early forties, he succeeded to the throne. He then married promptly—and wisely—but failed to produce the children for which all men hoped. After 1052 the problem of the succession became increasingly awkward.

Edward's exile had broken his insularity. As king he was partial to foreigners. He disliked Scandinavians, presumably because of his early experiences, but welcomed men from the western countries of Europe : Germans, Lotharingians, Flemings, French, Normans, and Bretons. Because of the subsequent Norman Conquest historians have sometimes been tempted to give special prominence to the Norman contingent. Yet in the church Normans were well outnumbered by Teutons, and among the laity Edward, when rewarding his kinsmen and friends, paid little attention to his mother's family. Edward was certainly close in his first years as king to Robert, abbot of Jumièges; but he had returned also with Lotharingian clerks, who likewise were rewarded; and in 1052 he sacrificed the unpopular Robert without, apparently, much of a pang. The only foreigner who obtained an earldom in England was Edward's nephew, Ralf, who was not a Norman but a son of the count of the Vexin. Even if the Normans in England worked in the interest of the duke —and there is little evidence for this—they were not recruited by Edward for that purpose. They were simply part of a foreign group in the household which the king, because of his long exile, chose to have around him, and whose members he sometimes rewarded with a benefice or fief in the country. The court, like the kingdom, remained Anglo-Danish in all essential features.

Harold, Godwin's son, earl of Wessex since 1053, typifies this amalgam. His father was descended from the lesser English nobility; his mother, Gytha, was a pure

Dane of more distinguished birth. We learn that the parents were ambitious for their children and carefully educated them to rule. Harold was trained as a soldier. We see him always in the company of housecarles and thegns, a relaxed and confident captain, an open and cheerful man, athletic, fond of women, rich, generous, a popular leader. His subsequent career shows that he himself was ambitious. All contemporaries agree that he was wise in the ways of the world, calculating and shrewd, never rash. He was not particularly religious. He founded a collegiate church and made a conventional pilgrimage to Rome; but he encroached on ecclesiastical lands and he prudently deferred making a Christian marriage until after he had obtained the throne. Yet he was a man whom no prelate shunned. Even St Wulfstan of Worcester was proud to have been his confessor. Men believed that he was basically well-intentioned and that as king he would make at least a conventional show of piety. Above all, he was recognized as a firm and just ruler. When he was Edward's second-in-command the kingdom was in safe hands.

The royal military forces had been reorganized by Alfred and his immediate successors in order to conquer the Danelaw. They created a navy and army and a defence system based on fortified boroughs. In the tenth century English military reputation stood at its peak. The kings had conquered East Anglia and Northumbria, smashed Norwegian invaders, advanced deep into Scotland, and overawed Wales. Then under Æthelred the English forces, erratically commanded and doubtful in their loyalty to their leader, had suffered humiliating reverses against new Danish invaders. The low morale was not completely exorcised before 1066. Cnut had relied mainly on his Danish army and navy and Edward had no need to train large military forces. Instead, the king and the earls, like their Danish predecessors, recruited professional escorts, mainly Scandinavian housecarles; and these, together with their English retainers, formed small private armies. Also Edward maintained until 1051 a small mercenary fleet. In an emergency, or for a great campaign, these cadres could be reinforced by calling out all men who had the duty to fight on land and sea. But since in Edward's reign there was little need for large armies, the ordinary soldiers, the thegns, were losing military experience and tradition.

Basically English military organization was not unlike the Norman. But there was a difference in method of fighting. Although the Anglo-Danish armies moved on horseback, they preferred to fight dismounted behind the shield-wall. In 1066 there were few, if any, true cavalry units in England. And for defence reliance was still placed on the fortified towns. Except on the Welsh marches the private castle was unknown in England. In 1066 the strength of English military power was a matter for speculation. It had not been tested for two generations.

The military system was, however, well designed for securing internal order. The only danger, and one largely avoided in Edward's reign, was civil war among the earls. England was undoubtedly the most peaceful and best governed kingdom in western Europe. To pay the mercenary forces Edward collected a tax, geld, from almost the whole of the kingdom. The coinage was exceptionally good. Justice was plentiful. Governmental techniques were well advanced : Edward was the only king to grant titles to land by means of a writ authenticated by a hanging two-sided seal. England had some of the characteristics of a civilized state. Edward was not, however, interested in the art of government or had any ambition except to enjoy the position he had belatedly acquired. The administration which he had inherited, and with the aid of his clerks repaired, was allowed to run on.

The English church was to be severely censured by the Norman conquerors. Even if we discount the prejudice of newcomers and the self-interest of those seeking to justify expropriation, there remains some justice in the Norman charges. Churches are always in need of reform, but, fortunately for them, are rarely put so ruthlessly at the bar as was the English church in 1070. By the end of Cnut's reign the great English tenth-century reformation was losing momentum. Men had become prosperous and worldly and the church was generally complacent. The founding of monasteries had almost come to an end.

Enough had been established. There were no glaring abuses in the church : it was more than respectable by the common European standard; but it was not a ministry of zealots. Moreover, it had some peculiarities, due to its Roman foundation, Celtic admixture, and long, rather isolated, history, which could be distasteful to strangers.

Edward did little to improve the tone. Despite his later reputation for sanctity, he does not seem to have been interested in church reform. He rewarded his favourite clerks with bishoprics and promoted a few monks. Some of these were able, some good men. He allowed a few ambitious prelates to accumulate several dioceses in plurality; and these were not always the worst bishops. He did little that was scandalous by the standards of the age. Although at the beginning of his reign he was occasionally suspected of simony, he made no practice of selling preferment. He seems to have enjoyed visits to his court by foreign abbots and towards the end of his life made atonement for his sins and provision for his burial by rebuilding Westminster abbey. He was an ordinary religious man. He had, however, no discernible ecclesiastical policy. The English church lacked guidance both from the king and from the archbishops whom he appointed to Canterbury.

The church, left to its own devices, became very uneven in quality. There were a few active centres of reform, as York and Worcester. Some monastic churches, for example the East-Anglian houses and Sherborne, at least maintained their reputation. Several collegiate churches were reformed by the imposition of a rule transforming a community of secular clerks into a body of canons living and sharing in common. At least one bishop moved his see into a more suitable church. But there was no co-ordinated reform. And the rapid decline at some hitherto famous churches was fatal to the reputation of the English church as a whole. Canterbury and Winchester, the leading monastic sees, were undoubtedly lax under Stigand, a secular clerk, who held them both together. The final blows to England's good name were Stigand's censure by the Roman see for taking Canterbury after Robert of Jumièges had been expelled and his failure to obtain an authentic pallium. The weaknesses of the English church were becoming, unfairly, notorious in Christendom.

The misunderstanding with Rome, common as such disagreements were in ecclesiastical history, was completely uncharacteristic of the Old-English church, for no church had had periods of greater illumination, no church had been more loyal to St Peter and the threshold of the apostles. The habit of pilgrimage to Rome was engrained in the English people. A free-will tribute to Rome, Peter's Pence, first instituted in the eighth or ninth century, was still being paid, even if sporadically. The English church, loyal while Rome had been corrupt, thought itself misunderstood when the reformed papacy became critical of its traditional ways and scandalized by an accidental irregularity.

Rome received with gratitude not only English pennies but also English works of art. English books and metalwork, indeed all English church furniture, mostly a product of the monasteries, were greatly prized in Europe. Foreigners in the English church usually sent some masterpiece as a present to their old home. The artistic activity of the monasteries continued in Edward's reign and there was a vast accumulation of treasure in the churches. The literary tradition was, however, weaker. There had been no true successor to Bede. The Anglo-Saxon Chronicle, annals in the vernacular, was still being written in some monasteries. Homiletic literature, again in Old-English, was being copied in a few centres, notably Worcester. But there was a lack of a true Latin culture. Although all monks and most bishops had studied Latin, the pastoral tradition was so strong in England that most writing was for the instruction of priests and their flocks, and hence usually in the native tongue. Because of this situation professional Latin authors were attracted to England. Two monks of St Bertin's in Flanders, Folcard and Goscelin, found English episcopal patrons and began their work of writing the lives of English saints. The eagerness with which they were welcomed by respectable English monasteries reveals that Latin scholarship was in short supply. Yet, paradoxically, it was not ignorance, but the unusual vernacular contribution that made the English church appear provincial and rustic, even unlearned, to those continental churches more Latin in tone.

Wealth and sophistication, tainted by supposed social, political, and ecclesiastical sickness, made England particularly open to the scorn of simpler and rougher peoples. England was, indeed, a natural victim for her aggressive neighbours. The imponderable factors in 1066 were how far the English military tradition had decayed, whether Harold, with no blood-right to kingship, could transfer loyalties to himself, and with what tenacity the people, if deprived of its captains, would fight against a foreign invader.

Chapter Five

The Invasion of England

OWING to the form of our sources the diplomacy which led to William's conquest of England is presented in distinct episodes. Whatever the nature of the exchanges of 1050–2 may have been, it was part of the Norman case that Edward confirmed his nomination of William as his heir by sending Earl Harold to him in 1064 so as to make the final arrangements for the duke's succession. And with this event, integral to the Norman justification and pictured on the Bayeux Tapestry, we reach the immediate prelude to the war. Although no English chronicler refers to Harold's embassy, the outline facts must be accepted, especially since the Tapestry, while in general agreement with William of Poitiers' narrative, gives its own version, a redaction specially edited for the people of Bayeux, with episodes and characters long forgotten but hardly invented for its viewers. Yet few English historians have accepted with full confidence Poitiers' interpretation of events. And it should not be overlooked that the Tapestry, although possibly following implicitly the common Norman tradition, does not go out of its way to stress the main theme of the chronicler.

The outlines of the case as given by William of Poitiers are as follows. Edward, as he reached the end of his life and mindful of his bequest of the throne to William, sent his most important vassal, Harold, earl of Wessex, to the duke to confirm the promise by oath and so bind himself to William that the succession would be unopposed. Harold escaped from some danger during the crossing and landed in the county of Ponthieu where Count Guy took him captive in the hope of a ransom. When William heard of this he obtained Harold's freedom through threats and rewards and entertained his guest honourably at Rouen. The duke then summoned a council to Bonne-ville-sur-Touques, near Lisieux, and Harold took the oath. According to the witness of many veracious and trustworthy men who were present, Harold of his own free will swore that he would be William's representative in King Edward's court and on the king's death would make every effort to secure the crown for William. In the mean-time he would hand over Dover castle, and such other castles as the duke would require him to build, to the duke's soldiers. William then took homage and fealty from Harold and confirmed his new vassal in all his English pos-sessions. In a later passage the chronicler informs us that Harold was also betrothed to one of William's daughters. After these ceremonies William took Harold on a cam-paign against Brittany, in which Harold demonstrated his strength, and, on their successful return, not only sent Harold back laden with gifts but also released his nephew, one of the hostages given in 1051.

In this story there are two main points : that Edward sent Harold to confirm his bequest of the kingdom and that Harold, in order to assure the bequest, became Wil-liam's vassal for his English estates. Neither point has been fully accepted by English historians. There has been an inclination to believe that Harold fell into William's clutches through misadventure and there has been general scepticism about the terms of the oath and the nature of the homage. The version conveyed by the Bayeux Tapes-try must be considered before an opinion is expressed. This embroidery, it is believed, was commissioned by Odo, bishop of Bayeux and earl of Kent, the Conqueror's half-brother, to decorate the cathedral church he had rebuilt and which was dedicated in 1077. Whether the designer and the workshops were English or Norman is still dis-puted. But it is not unlikely that the work was done at Canterbury. The theme of the Tapestry is that a great hero, Harold, by breaking the oath he had taken on the relics of Bayeux and also by forgetting William's benefits, came to ruin, not ignominiously, but as a hero struggling against heaven's fate.

According to the Tapestry, Harold sailed from Bosham in Sussex. If we accept this detail Harold was almost cer-

tainly sailing for Normandy or Brittany and was driven
off course by a south-west wind. If he had been bound for
anywhere but the north-west coast of France he would
surely have crossed from Dover. The Tapestry differs
from the chronicler in placing the feudal homage and
then the oath on the relics after the Breton campaign, and
the oath is expressly located at Bayeux. The Tapestry
occasionally alters the chronological sequence in the interests of the design or of drama. And here we may have
another example of this practice. But as the Norman case
turned so much on Harold's oath it is strange that Poitiers
should locate it at Bonneville (a place he knew), the Tapestry at Bayeux, and Orderic Vital, a twelfth-century writer
but well informed, at Rouen. This problem cannot be
solved. Bayeux is off the main route from Rouen to Mont
St Michel, but does not involve a great detour. Perhaps
relics from Bayeux were taken to Bonneville. Perhaps an
oath was taken at Bonneville on the way to Brittany and
a second time at Bayeux as William accompanied his de-
parting guest to the coast. But the uncertainty suggests
that the oath was not originally the central feature which
it later assumed.

The oath on relics was an undertaking to God. The
homage and fealty bound Harold to the duke. The desire
of a claimant was always to be put in possession, to be
given seisin, as early as possible, and especially during the
lifetime of the benefactor. Geoffrey of Anjou demanded
in 1135 that King Henry I, his father-in-law, should put
him in possession of his wife's dowry and allow him to take
the homage of the Norman barons so as to secure his
succession to the duchy. Henry refused and Geoffrey had
to conquer Normandy from Stephen. When Stephen in
1153 accepted Geoffrey's son, Henry Plantagenet, as his
heir and successor in England it was agreed that Stephen's
son, William, should hold his English fiefs of Henry, and
that all the leading vassals of each party should do homage to the rival leader, saving their fealty to Stephen. In
the light of these later examples we can see clearly the
meaning of the Norman story about Harold. Yet the problem of whether the story is true remains.

Within two years of these events, on the death of Edward, William presented his case to the greater European powers, including the pope and emperor, and probably in the form that we have been discussing. It is not completely inconceivable that William fabricated his two main points —the bequest of the throne in 1050–1 and Harold's embassy. Philip Augustus concocted an imaginary case in the thirteenth century to present to the pope against King John. But it is more likely that William used historical facts which were common knowledge and gave them the meaning which suited his purpose. This was the safest procedure. We also know that William and the papal court deceived each other over their true intentions in 1066. There is every reason to believe that diplomacy could be subtle in the eleventh century. William was cunning and was scheming for high stakes. So also was Harold. According to the earl's panegyrist he was adroit, intelligent, and prudent, a man who could wonderfully dissemble his purpose; he pressed on to his goal but always enjoyed himself on the way; he passed through ambushes with mocking caution; he was, alas, too ready with his oaths. He studied in person French politics and got to know the leading men so well that he could not be deceived by their proposals. We should be prepared to believe that in 1064 one open and one covert claimant to the English throne probed each other's intentions and sought to get the maximum advantage out of ambiguous acts. When in 1066 the pope sent, and William accepted, a papal banner, Alexander II and Cardinal Hildebrand hoped that the duke was conquering England as a papal vassal, an intention far from William's mind. In 1064 when William received Harold's fealty he established a relationship which could be exploited. Harold, on his side, may have been derisively eluding Norman ambushes and taking pleasure in deceiving his host. These conjectures cannot be proved, may indeed be wrong, but at least they are based on the characters which contemporaries gave to the two main actors.

There is no evidence that Harold on his return to England busied himself on William's behalf. Such evidence as there is suggests that he cunningly advanced his own interests. In the autumn of 1065, Harold's younger brother, Tostig, earl of Northumbria, was driven out of his earldom by an armed revolt and we are informed that he accused Harold in the king's court of instigating the conspiracy. Harold cleared himself of the charge by an oath, but he disobeyed the king's order to restore Tostig by force of arms and allowed Morkere, the brother of Edwin, earl of Mercia, to take the earldom. Shortly afterwards Harold married their sister. It looks as though Harold deliberately removed a possible rival or opponent and by aiding and allying with the Mercian family assured himself of the support of all the major earls in England. The king was distracted by these events. Tostig was his favourite, and when he was forced to banish him he contracted the sickness of mind from which he soon died.

Tostig was exiled before Christmas 1065. Invitations had already been sent out for a great court to be held at Westminster at Christmas when the abbey church that Edward had built was to be consecrated. We may assume that both archbishops, most of the bishops, many abbots, and all the leading nobility were at court while Edward lay on his death-bed. The abbey church of Westminster was dedicated on 28 December, in Edward's unavoidable absence, and the king died a week later, on the fourth or fifth of January 1066. The English magnates had plenty of time to make plans. From future events it is unmistakably clear that, whatever their undertakings to William may have been, they had no wish to have a foreign king. To the best of our knowledge they agreed unanimously that Harold, Edward's brother-in-law, should succeed. Moreover, although it has sometimes been disputed, there is every reason to believe that Edward in his dying moments nominated Harold as his successor. William of Poitiers admits this aspect of Harold's case several times. It was a damaging admission to make and proves that the fact could not be denied. The anonymous author of the *Vita Ædwardi*, who gives us a graphic account of Edward's last hours, can be understood in the same sense. The Bayeux Tapestry shows Edward on his death-bed offering his hand to a man who is usually understood to be Harold. The English chroniclers believed that Harold had received Edward's dying bequest.

Edward may have been persuaded; but it cannot be

claimed that Harold packed the bedchamber. There were present Queen Edith, Earl Godwin's daughter, who was believed to be a supporter of William, Robert fitzWimarch, a Norman or Breton, and Harold and Archbishop Stigand of Canterbury, one of Harold's adherents. It is also probably true that Edward was out of his mind. But this circumstance, which today would invalidate a will, in the eleventh century only gave the testament greater force. Edward had roused himself from a long coma just before he died and claimed that he had had visions. Such closeness to heaven gave his last words profound authority. So Edward died; and on the morrow, 6 January, he was buried and Harold was crowned king.

The haste was prudent and should not be considered indecorous or as indicating a coup d'état. Edward himself, the nominated successor to his half-brother, Harthacnut, had been chosen as king by all the people in London before his predecessor's burial. But by receiving consecration from Archbishop Stigand, Harold gave another advantage to his Norman rival. Stigand, without an authentic pallium, was not acknowledged to have metropolitan powers. Indeed because of the uncanonical way in which he had succeeded to Canterbury and other irregularities even his episcopal ministrations were suspect in some quarters. From Harold's standpoint everything had gone well. He had succeeded to the throne without opposition, possibly by common consent, and had been consecrated king. All he had to do was to withstand his rivals. And clearly he was confident that he could do so. He had taken their measure and was not overawed. On the Tapestry the coronation scene has a central position. King Harold sitting on his throne in majesty, adorned with crown, orb, and sceptre, and with the sword of state held at his side, receives the acclamation of the people. Duke William had been completely defrauded of his expectations.

It is difficult to say whether William had seriously expected to be invited by the English magnates on Edward's death to occupy the vacant throne. He knew that Edward, almost as much a stranger, had been summoned from Normandy to England in similar circumstances. But he was probably not so confident as to be unaware that there was one important difference. Edward was King Æthelred's lawful son, a claimant who had been kept out of his rightful inheritance by Scandinavian invaders. In William's veins ran no drop of English royal blood. Moreover, as the son of a count and a tanner's daughter there was little in his lineage to recommend him to English earls. Yet he may well have expected his rival to come from the English royal family, say Æthelred's great-grandson, Edgar the Ætheling, and he seems to have been genuinely disappointed by Harold's treachery.

It is also difficult to be sure how much William believed in the legal case that his supporters provided. In fact they made a most skilful appreciation of the issues, and by accepting that there was a clash of rights—that William's claim was based on one set of arguments and Harold's on another—they argued persuasively. The duke relied on the bequest of 1050-1, confirmed in 1064, the earl on the codicil *in articulo mortis*. Harold's nomination was not only more recent, and so probably a valid revocation of earlier dispositions, but also, since it came from the dying testator, the more solemn. This difficulty the Normans countered by pleading the nullity of the codicil owing to Harold's prior engagements to William. He was not in a position to receive the bequest since it made him a perjurer and a faithless vassal. The act was void. There was also the further problem to the Norman lawyer that Harold had acquired the legal advantages of the possessor. He had been elected, crowned, and anointed king, had received the plaudits of the people, and had effectively wielded the royal powers. It was always difficult in feudal law to remove a lawful possessor. The Norman plea, therefore, was that Harold was an unlawful possessor. Not only had he the disabilities already mentioned, but he had seized the throne without an election and had been crowned by an archbishop condemned by the papacy. He was not a true king but a cruel tyrant whom any rightminded person, especially the lawful claimant, had the duty to destroy. William of Poitiers sums up the Norman attitude in a sorrowful but condemnatory obituary notice which he inserted in his book after describing Harold's ignominious burial: 'Now you shine no longer in the crown which in breach of faith you usurped, you sit no more on the throne to which through pride you climbed. Your doom proves how lawfully you were raised up by Edward's dying gift.'

William had a case and he was prepared to enforce his claim by war. In reality he had to fight against a king in full possession of his kingdom. On the Bayeux Tapestry it is always *Haroldus rex*, and William of Poitiers, except when pleading, recognized Harold's title. Nor did the Normans underestimate the new king. Poitiers certainly builds up Harold in order to increase William's achievement, but there are many indications that the Norman barons viewed the invasion of England as a dangerous gamble and that William regarded it as a major undertaking. Against English wealth and the English naval and military forces (sometimes derided as devoid of a victorious tradition, sometimes described as innately savage, but always respected), and against the strong and daring Harold meticulous preparations were required.

Speed too was essential. Edward's death occurred at a time not unfavourable for William. Summer and autumn were the campaigning seasons and a calm Channel crossing was necessary. If Edward had died a month or two earlier it would have been better; but if William decided to invade during July, which is likely, he still had six months for his preparations. He had to attack in 1066. To leave the expedition until the following year would give Harold time to consolidate and the Normans time to get cold feet. William had three military tasks : to recruit an army, to assemble a navy, and to protect the duchy during his absence. To aid him in these affairs and also to enlist the active sympathy or at least the benevolent neutrality of other princes William mounted a diplomatic offensive as well. In the first place he probably required Harold to surrender the throne and, on the possessor's refusal, drew up a legal claim in substance like that given us by the Norman chroniclers, especially William of Poitiers. This tractate could be used in negotiations with other powers. It demonstrated that William had a just right to the English kingdom and that Harold was a faithless vassal of the duke and a perjured usurper.

As William enlisted soldiers from Brittany and Aquitaine he must have come to terms with their rulers. Eustace, count of Boulogne, was probably anxious to take part, but, as Edward's brother-in-law and a possible claimant, he was required to give his son as hostage. The Count of Flanders, regent of France and the young king's guardian, was William's father-in-law and could be expected to favour the enterprise. Ambassadors were also sent farther afield. Svein of Denmark is said to have given them a friendly reception. He probably knew that his old rival Harold Hardrada, king of Norway, was likewise making preparations to invade England, and, himself a claimant, may well have hoped that the Norman and Norwegian would tire each other out and give him his chance later. The Emperor Henry IV, or the regency, was also claimed as a supporter of William, but it is hard to see what advantage Germany saw in a Norman victory.

The most important of William's distant negotiations, however, were with the pope. We have no firm record of this secret diplomacy; but William's envoy, the archdeacon of Lisieux, offered, probably, that the duke would reform the English church and resume payment of Peter's Pence, possibly—although there must have been some ambiguity—that William would hold his conquest as a papal fief. We know that the papal court was divided and that Cardinal Hildebrand, later Pope Gregory VII, was the duke's champion. Whether the offer of vassalage was a condition imposed by Hildebrand or a dishonest proposal of the archdeacon, it was proclaimed symbolically when Alexander II sent William a flag and tacitly accepted when William decided to fight under the banner. Probably at the time William thought that the papal blessing was well worth a promise which might have to be broken. Harold was foresworn and William need God on his side. He ordered the Norman monasteries pray for his success, and, when he landed in England, wore, hanging from his neck, the relics on which Har had taken his oath. Firm belief in the justice of his ca confidence that God and his saints and his vicar on earth were fighting for him, nerved the duke and his a in this dangerous undertaking.

William was supported throughout the campaign by his half-brothers Robert, count of Mortain, and Odo, bishop of Bayeux. Although William of Malmesbury considered Robert a stupid fool, the two formed the duke's inner military council. The expeditionary force must have been recruited by invitation. William held several meetings with his vassals and persuaded them to support the adventure; but he would not have wished to denude the duchy of barons and soldiers and his task was to enlist suitable mercenaries. The Norman barons seem usually to have contributed one member of their family as a squadron commander—often a son—and sent him with some of their own feudal troops. For example, among the eleven nobles whom William of Poitiers lists as present at the battle of Hastings, at least four were representing their fathers. Robert of Beaumont, whom Poitiers mentions specially for his fine work on the right wing of the army, was that day fighting in his first battle. The Norman barons acted prudently. If we may judge from the order of battle at Hastings no more than a third of the invading army was composed of Normans. The largest foreign contingent came probably from Brittany, for it was an area rich in poor knights, and Bretons formed the bulk of the left wing at Hastings. Troops were recruited also from Maine, Aquitaine, Flanders, and 'France', and these made up William's right in the battle. Foot soldiers, especially archers and a few crossbowmen and engineers, were engaged as well, but we are not told from where. Besides the active combatants there was the army of squires, valets, purveyors, and camp-followers whom William could control less successfully than the soldiers.

Equally important was a fleet. We can assume that William impressed and hired such boats as were available. Many of the leading nobles promised a quota of ships. But the numbers required were large, for William had decided to throw his troops across the Channel in a single wave and also without deliberate diversionary strikes. This plan suggests that William thought he had no troops to spare. Ships were accordingly built in Normandy, and presumably modified too in order to carry horses. The Tapestry shows in lively scenes the assembly of the stores on the beaches—the ships, hauberks, helmets, swords, lances, and axes, the skins and hogsheads of wine and the sacks of provisions. A medieval army was always prepared to live by plundering, but the answer of a defender was to scorch the countryside; and in any case a French army would not fight well on beer or water.

By August William was ready to move. He had set up a council of regency under his wife, Matilda, and Roger of Beaumont, and he was leaving behind several young children to represent his line should he, like his father, fail to return from his adventures. He was about to set in motion a military exercise such as had hardly been attempted before in the north : the large-scale transport of cavalry, together with their mounts, across a sizable stretch of sea. For the Vikings horses had been a luxury, something to capture if they could. In any case they did not fight as cavalry. But for the Normans their chargers were essential, and any invasion plan had to make provision for their transport. That horses could be successfully carried was probably well known. A Viking army had crossed from Boulogne to Lympne in 892 taking their horses with them. The Byzantine navy was accustomed to transport cavalry and had specialized ships for the purpose. In 1038 it had carried Scandinavian mercenaries, under Harold Hardrada, now king of Norway, and Norman knights across the Straits of Messina in an attempt to conquer Sicily from the Muslims. And in 1060-1 the Normans in Italy themselves, using local ships and crews, had made several successful landings in the neighbourhood of Messina, starting with reconnaissance parties and finishing with a full invasion force of cavalry. There was much traffic between the Normans in Italy and those at home and William must have heard of the successful invasion of Sicily. It is even possible that there were Normans from Italy in his army. But given the idea, his men could probably provide the technical means. Horses are a fragile cargo, but they can easily be boxed or roped.

William's forces were assembled round the estuary of the Dives. We are not told what strategic plans he had made and, indeed, we are very ill-informed about the planning of medieval campaigns. In the absence of maps and the whole paraphernalia of military intelligence as later understood, strategic planning must have been very simple. We can assume that William and his advisers were familiar with the legend of their ancestors' conquest of Normandy and had some knowledge of the campaigns of Svein and Cnut and other Scandinavian adventurers in England and of the Norman invasion of Sicily. He must have had sailors who knew the southern English ports and probably guides who could have led him to some of the major towns. Accordingly the only plan open to William was to make a beach landing, establish a bridge-head, try to capture towns by raids on land and by sea, and exploit the situation as it opened up before him. An invader with small and mobile forces hardly had the need to make detailed plans. If he were repulsed from one beach he could stand off and try again. This was to happen when Tostig invaded England in May. But William was invading with a cumbersome fleet loaded with horses. He could not hit and run and he could not keep indefinitely on the move. It seems that for him the choice of the place to land was a basic decision. Further, as William assembled his forces on the Dives we can infer that he intended to make a direct crossing of the Channel and land somewhere round Southampton Water. Edward had made a similar expedition, it seems, in 1035–6, landing at or near Southampton. In May 1066 Tostig successfully raided the Isle of Wight. And as Harold then set up his personal headquarters on the Isle it is clear that he also expected William's attack to be in that sector.

Apart from the disadvantage of the longest ferry such a plan was probably the best that William could make. If he could seize the Isle of Wight he obtained the most useful bridge-head open to him. He could raid by land up to Winchester and then to the Thames and he could widen the landing by sea-borne raids along the coast. Thus, if he had a simple strategic plan it was probably to raid, and possibly occupy before winter, the south-eastern shires of England. From Southampton Water he could move in many directions. At the worst, the Ise of Wight and some of the hinterland could probably be held with ease during the winter in preparation for a new invasion in 1067.

If this was the original plan it miscarried. William's forces were detained for a month around the River Dives by adverse winds. This must have been the most trying time for the Norman commanders. A large miscellaneous army had to be paid and provisioned and also kept under strict discipline while the precious weeks slipped by. In September William moved his ships, or saw them driven by a westerly gale, up the coast to St Valery, in the territory of that Guy, count of Ponthieu, who had captured Harold. This transfer, whether planned, opportunist, or involuntary, was costly. Ships were lost, and their crews buried in secrecy, and some troops deserted. Only a brilliant commander could have rallied his bored and discouraged army. And there was further disappointment, for even at St Valery the wind was wrong. The body of the saint was taken out of the church and carried round the town while the soldiers prayed for a favourable breeze. On 27 September the wind backed south and in the evening William embarked his troops. They were bound for the Cinque Ports.

This plan, if it was a substitute for the other, would seem to be inferior in general strategic scope. On the other hand, as so much time had been lost, it can be considered a necessary narrowing of the objective. Its one advantage was the shortening of the sea crossing. But had this been a serious consideration William could have coasted still farther north to Boulogne, and it must be inferred that the distance of the ferry did not dictate William's plans. The obvious disadvantages were that the Normans had to attack a sector, studded with ports, notoriously loyal to Harold's family, and that, as the coastal strip was backed by the great forest of Andred, the beach-head would be narrow and difficult to exploit. Unless everything that happened took place according to William's plan—an inconceivable result—the invasion would seem to have been reduced to little more than a probe limited in objective to the capturing of the Cinque Ports and preparing for a more extensive campaign in the following year.

The time of William's embarkation was decided by the wind, not by military intelligence. But, had he known, the situation was for the moment good. Harold, after his coronation, had first secured the allegiance of all the king-dom and then made preparations to defend it. Between February and May 'Halley's' comet flared in the sky, understood by all as a portent of war, but giving no clear pointer to the victor. As the comet disappeared, Harold's brother, Tostig, raided from Flanders, but was every-where successfully repulsed by local forces and was obliged to coast north to Scotland. Harold knew that William was making military preparations and he prob-ably soon heard that Harold Hardrada, king of Norway, was sailing south, by way of Shetland and Orkney, with a hostile fleet. He left the defence of the north to the brother earls, Edwin and Morkere, and he and his brothers, Gyrth and Leofwine, prepared to defend the south. Harold apparently mobilized his forces immedi-ately after Tostig's raid. He stationed an army, or army groups, along the southern coast and himself took com-mand of the fleet which he based on the Isle of Wight. Reconnaissance parties or spies were sent to Normandy and it is likely that each commander was fairly well in-formed of the other's actions and plans.

But William's misfortunes were also Harold's. The westerly gales in September which transferred the duke's fleet to St Valery also drove the king's through the Channel to the Thames, and Harold's naval losses seem to have been greater than William's. Moreover, the delays which caused William some desertions appear to have lost Harold most of the local defence forces. Early in Sep-tember both the Norman invaders and the English de-fenders were in some disorder. Although Harold was prob-ably in the worse plight he clearly still had the advantage, for the campaigning season was drawing to a close and William had not sailed.

It was at this time that Harold Hardrada reached the Tyne and received Tostig as a welcome reinforcement. The Norwegian fleet, estimated at some three to five hun-dred ships, sailed up the Humber and Ouse and at Riccall disembarked an army which marched on York. On 20 September they heavily defeated Earls Edwin and Morkere at Gate Fulford and passed through the city to camp on the River Derwent at Stamford Bridge. King

Harold was already riding north with his army. On 25 September he too pushed through York and then threw himself on the Viking encampment. In a savage battle, of which we have few details, he slew Harold Hardrada, Tostig, and an Irish king, and then allowed the remnants to withdraw. Thus when William set sail for England on 27 September all the English leaders were in the north, Edwin and Morkere re-forming their armies and Harold resting his at York.

William's fleet made an unmolested night crossing and in the morning the army disembarked on the Sussex coast near Pevensey. The towns of Pevensey and Hastings seem to have surrendered without a fight, and at the latter, perhaps at both, a motte and bailey castle was thrown up in order to protect the encampment. In the fortnight which elapsed before the battle of Hastings William and his men seem to have done little except to create and fortify a small bridge-head. They undertook some reconnaissance, but do not seem to have pushed eastwards into Kent or westwards into Hampshire. They were, as has been said, in a constricted position under the downs and the great forest, and were isolated from news. William was probably at a loss what to do. According to William of Poitiers the duke received first a message from Robert fitz-Wimarch, and then an ambassador from Harold. Robert, a kinsman of both the late king and the duke, who had held an important post at Edward's court, sent contemptuous advice.

> King Harold has just fought with his own brother and with the king of Norway—considered to be the most powerful warrior under the sun—and in a single battle has killed them both and wiped out their enormous armies. Encouraged by this success he is now advancing with all speed and with a strong and numerous army against you. In my opinion against Harold your troops are worth no more than despicable dogs. You are said to be a sensible man and so far in both peace and war you have behaved sensibly. So I advise you to act with prudence now, lest rashness causes you to throw your-

self into a danger from which you cannot escape. Stay within your castles and for the time being avoid battle.

The duke replied to the messenger :

Take back my thanks to your lord for his advice to be prudent—although advice without the insults would have been more seemly—and take back also this message: I shall not remain on the defensive within entrenchments and walls but will fight with Harold as soon as possible. And I am confident that, even if I had only ten-thousand men as good as the sixty-thousand that I have brought with me, through their courage and with the help of God he and his army will be destroyed.

William, of course, had not 60,000 men in his army. It is doubtful whether he could have brought 10,000. The Normans using ships which could carry about twenty soldiers and their mounts had transported, in several waves, up to 1,000 cavalry across the Straits of Messina for the victorious campaign of 1061. According to the designer of the Bayeux Tapestry William too had ships as large, and so we must allow fifty ships for each thousand cavalry. There were also the servants, the infantry, and the stores. Whatever the exact size of William's army, Robert fitz-Wimarch's message, although bringing information that was badly needed, cannot have given much comfort. And William in fact remained within or near his fortifications until forced out of them.

The messages exchanged between Robert and William appear to have a smack of truth. The exchanges reported by Poitiers between Harold and William seem much more like a literary exercise. Poitiers makes each rival rehearse his claim to the throne and William offer to take his case to court to be heard by English or Norman law. Alternatively William offered the *duellum*, the ordeal by battle, with each claimant fighting in person. It is not impossible that William tried such manoeuvres. More likely each defied the other and protested the justice of his cause. Be that as it may, Harold's final response was at least in character. When a monk of Fécamp, William's envoy, pressed for an answer Harold wasted no words : 'We march straight on', he said; and then, 'We march to victory.'

Harold had left York on hearing of William's invasion and had retraced his steps down the Great North Road to London. There he waited for about a week, perhaps hoping that the northern earls would rejoin him. But finally he pushed on with his brothers, Earls Gyrth and Leofwine, to close with the invaders. Harold was making forced marches as rapid and bold as those he had made against Wales. According to William of Poitiers the king, enraged by the devastations committed by the Normans round their camp, had resolved to make a night, or at least a sudden, attack on the bridge-head and had posted a vast navy to cut off the Normans' retreat by sea. This may, indeed, have been Harold's plan. He had just now successfully used it against the Vikings in the north, and clearly was not overawed by the Normans. The select core of his army, the professional housecarles and the personal retinues of himself and his brothers—their thegns and household troops—were possibly tired after their long rides and their short battle, but they must have been in good heart, and it is doubtful whether Harold needed more men. He probably agreed with William that in battle quality counted more than numbers. It is true that in the battle itself, if an independent or reserve force could have been thrown in at one of the critical moments, this could have made all the difference. But it is unlikely that such a tactical refinement was part of Harold's plan. We can probably assume that Harold was prepared to deliver battle. Nevertheless, we cannot be sure that he intended to fight regardless of the tactical situation. To bring his forces up closer to the enemy and also prevent him from slipping away by sea gave Harold every advantage. At one extreme William could have been starved out. It must be recognized that the duke was most uncomfortably placed in a very shallow bridge-head. The initiative lay entirely with Harold.

In the event William snatched it from him. Harold emerged from the forest covering Hastings in the evening of 13 October and decided to rest his army. He halted at a deserted place remembered by the English as near the grey apple tree and by the Normans as Senlac, a corruption of *sand-lac*, the sandy brook. Both commanders sent out scouts and made their plans. William had only a narrow choice. He could either wait to be attacked or go into the attack. Like the good general he was, he chose to advance. Early next morning he heard mass, hung the relics on which Harold had sworn round his neck, ordered his troops to arm, and briefly addressed his commanders. He reminded the Normans of the victories they had already won under his leadership. He reminded all nations of their homelands and exploits. He said it was do or die for they were surrounded. He told them not to be frightened by the numbers of the enemy, for skill and valour were the essentials and the English had a poor reputation as soldiers. Finally he reminded them that they fought in a just cause and that God would not forsake them. The Norman army then marched out of its encampment to give battle. And, as though by a miracle, William gained the initiative, for he found Harold's army unprepared. Possibly the English had thought that the Normans would not dare to attack. William had forced Harold's hand, and the king, with no choice except to fight or retreat, called in his men and prepared to receive the assault.

The only early descriptions of the battle of Hastings are by William of Poitiers and the designer of the Bayeux Tapestry, both working a decade after the event. William's biographer was not present, but he was in a position to learn from those who were; and as he had been a knight before he entered the church and was familiar with William's campaigns he was unlikely to get his detail wrong. Moreover, although not impartial, he had no desire to belittle the enemy. Odo of Bayeux, for whom it is thought the Tapestry was made, was in the thick of the fight. As both these sources are in general agreement we have an account in which we can put some faith. Poitiers cannot be trusted, however, in his estimate of the size of the armies, which he put at scores of thousands. The Norman striking force must have been smaller than the invasion army, and modern observers have usually agreed that each leader had about 7,000 troops under command on the day. Yet even these figures may be too high. It tends to be assumed, because of the importance of the battle, that the armies were large. But two considerations should be borne in mind. Harold's army must have been small—the remnants of the forces that he had just taken to York and back, reinforced by the army of at least one brother and by the troops gradually coming in to join his standard—and the Norman army was no larger and may, as some believed, have been smaller. Moreover, as it is unlikely that the duke of Normandy or the king of England usually took on campaign more than a few hundred troops, armies of 4,000 would be memorable.

If we can trust the Bayeux Tapestry, the equipment of both armies was basically the same and each was equally well accoutred. A battle between veteran generals commanding comparable armies in contrasting style is always of interest to a student of the art of war. But what gives Hastings exceptional interest is that clearly both leaders had made a deep tactical analysis before the engagement. It is true that Harold's tactics in the battle were largely dictated by the swiftness of the Norman advance, but it is likely that the king, having accompanied William on his Breton campaign, had decided, failing a surprise attack on the Norman camp, to counter light feudal cavalry by a defensive infantry phalanx. Such a formation, especially if aided by the ground, was almost impregnable to horse-men armed with spear and sword and with their mounts completely unprotected; and the defenders could turn to the offensive when losses had so weakened and dis-couraged the attackers that they withdrew in disorder. But William was probably prepared for these tactics and had planned to defeat them. He had engaged a force of infan-try and especially archers; and although it seems that he handled this arm, doubtless from lack of experience, without much assurance or skill, infantry equipped with long-range missiles, supported by cavalry, was the true answer to an infantry mass armed with short-range weapons.

Scouts kept the two generals informed of each other's movements, but the French were still unprepared for what they were to see when, after moving out of their camp at Hastings, they got their first sight of Harold's army. The Anglo-Danish forces were massed around a hill, and once they had taken up position the immobility and discipline of the housecarles and thegns was to remain a matter for wonder among the victors. William then deployed his troops, apparently at leisure and unharassed by English skirmishers. He sent forward light and heavy infantry, mostly bowmen (Poitiers claims that there were some crossbowmen, but they are not shown on the Tapestry), and supported them with squadrons of cavalry. He himself was in the centre with his Norman troops; on the left were mainly Bretons and on the right the other French auxiliaries. The attack failed. The archers, perhaps pressed by the impatient cavalry, must have got too close for they were crushed by the weight of the English missiles—spears of all sorts, throwing-axes, a few arrows, and stones tied to sticks. The cavalry passed through them, threw their javelins and then attacked the shield-wall with swords. The whole armies were engaged and the fighting was bitter. It was now, according to the Tapestry, that Harold's two brothers, Gyrth and Leofwine, were killed. But the attack was contained. Norman shields and armour gave little protection against the two-handed battle-axe, and missiles thrown from the rear rained upon the attackers. The charge lost its momentum; the squadrons wavered; and all, infantry and cavalry, led by the Bretons on the left, turned away, pursued by some English troops, who thought that the battle was won. William was probably unhorsed—he had three chargers killed under him during the battle—and it was believed that he was dead. But he lived to save the day. Almost carried away by the troops streaming down the hill, the duke, with bared head, shouting that he was alive, beat back his men and not only stopped the panic but rallied enough cavalry to cut off, surround, and destroy the English pursuers.

William of Poitiers was probably right in believing that the duke's coolness and determination snatched victory out of defeat. For, as the poet wrote in *Beowulf*, 'unless he is already doomed, fortune is apt to favour the man who

keeps his nerve.' Harold had been offered his best opportunity for a general charge and had let it slip. If he had
got all his men into movement the weight would surely
have broken the last coherence of the invading army. But
indecision, stubbornness in a prepared plan, caution, or
sheer inability to inspire his shocked troops, left him standing and again waiting. William was allowed to reorganize
and attack how and when he pleased. He sent in a second
charge, and although the right wing, and especially the
squadron under Robert of Beaumont, fought well, and
breaches were made in the shield-wall, the very pressure
of the attack helped the English to close their ranks and
the congestion was so severe that even the dead could not
fall to the ground. The Normans were again forced to turn
away and this time may deliberately have drawn some of
the English on in order to butcher them in the open, a
stratagem used at Messina and Arques and which now the
cavalry repeated several times. William had taken the
measure of the English. He sent squadron after squadron
against the dwindling phalanx and used his archers more
wisely. It became, indeed, as Poitiers wrote, a strange
battle in which while one side was in constant motion the
other stood as though rooted to the ground. In the English
host the dead moved more than the living.

Towards the end of the afternoon the English army
could fight no more. Many of the commanders had fallen
and among them the king himself. Exactly when and how
Harold died the Normans did not know. The king's body,
mutilated and hard to recognize, was found much later
among the heaps of the slain. More distant writers, perhaps interpreting a doubtful passage of the Bayeux Tapestry, believed that Harold had been struck by an arrow
in the eye. With the king's death his army took to flight
and the French went in pursuit, their horses' hooves exact-
ing a last punishment on the fallen. But the battle was not
quite over. Some English rallied where the uneven ground
favoured them, and Count Eustace of Boulogne, hard
pressed and urging the duke to sound the retreat, received
such a blow between his shoulders as he uttered the
cowardly words that blood gushed from his nose and

mouth and he had to be carried away. The duke saved the situation again, but the rash pursuit had been costly. Some of his most famous soldiers were killed in this final skirmish.

There seems to have been no great rejoicing among the victors. Their losses had been heavy and, although they had won a hard-fought battle, the strategic and political gains were at first hard to see. To win a battle was not to win a campaign. To win a campaign was not to conquer the country. An old soldier, familiar with Viking lore, counted his blessings and prepared to fight again. But when the bodies of Harold and his brothers were found among the dead, William, even in his lassitude, must have sensed that he had won a victory which might unlock all doors.

All our descriptions of the battle come from the winning side and Poitiers was committed to enlarging William's part. But there seems to be no drastic distortion. The only cowards were the Bretons and later Count Eustace. The Normans, of course, fought well, but none were stauncher than Harold's troops. For Poitiers, God gave victory to the side with the just cause. The writer was fully aware of the clash of two styles of fighting, but he does not explicitly blame the defender's tactics. Unable to comment on Harold's leadership, he praises William's courage rather than his skill. The duke was often in the thick of the fighting and sometimes in great danger, but he was always in command. He was the true architect of the victory. And no one would wish to dispute this view. Harold was out-generalled. His apparent inflexibility may have been heroic, but a good leader lives to fight again. Perhaps death caught him before he felt the need to disengage. Perhaps he waited for an expected relieving force too long. Perhaps he grew tired, dispirited, and ceased to think. But with his death fell not only a king with a disputed title but a nation as well.

William of Malmesbury, writing his *Gesta Regum Anglorum* in 1124–5, closed his Second Book with the battle of Hastings. He explained that Harold had few soldiers with him except mercenaries, but went on to remark :

In saying this I do not disparage the valour of the Normans, in whom, because of their race and deeds, I have every confidence. But I think that those who exaggerate the numbers of the English and underrate their courage make a mistake, for by taking this line, far from covering the Normans with praise, they smirch them with shame. What a wonderful tribute it is to an unconquered race to suggest that they conquered men who were hampered by their unwieldy numbers and faint-hearted because of their cowardice—rather than an enemy few but eager to fight and ready to lay down their lives and die for their fatherland.

After the battle William buried his own dead and gave the English permission to remove theirs. He refused, however, to surrender Harold's body to the queen-mother, who begged for it and would even have paid for it, but entrusted it to William Malet for burial. The Normans jested that Harold should be put as guardian of that sea and shore which he had defended so well, and believed that he was indeed buried on the shore near William's encampment; the English soon produced more romantic stories. William was certainly wise in denying to the conquered a tomb which could have become the centre of a dangerous cult; but if he also denied Christian burial to his rival he may be thought to have been a little ungenerous.

To win a battle like Hastings was to gain at least some weeks in which to exploit it. William knew that the northern earls were in arms and he was aware that no one had yet made voluntary submission to him. Therefore, as soon as he had received reinforcements, he moved fast to secure the south-eastern shires, advancing by way of Romney, which he punished for destroying a part of the invasion force which had gone astray, to Dover, which, chastened by the example, prepared to submit. It was, however, set on fire by the Norman army. William spent a week at Dover, strengthening its fortifications, and resting those of his troops who had gone down with dysentery. Canterbury, equally impressed, surrendered and was spared. But then William fell ill. The exploitation was losing momentum and the English were rallying. In London were gathered the most important men, Archbishops Stigand and Ealdred, Earls Edwin and Morkere and Edgar the Ætheling, a direct descendant of King Æthelred through Edmund Ironside and Edward the Exile, but only a boy and handicapped by foreign birth. Edgar had apparently been completely ignored on King Edward's death; but now he was the only claimant who might possibly rally the English, and it was decided, apparently on Ealdred's initiative, to make him king. But before the coronation William was on the move again, the English magnates hesitated, and then the earls refused to fight. The duke attacked the suburbs south of London Bridge and set them on fire. But the city itself remained hostile. So William, still ravaging, pushed up the Thames to Wallingford, where Archbishop Stigand made his submission. This defection was both a straw in the wind and a great reinforcement. Emboldened, William crossed the Thames and approached London from the north-west. At Berkhamsted the leading men came out, submitted to William, and surrendered the city. They were Archbishop Ealdred, Bishops Wulfstan of Worcester and Walter of Hereford, Earls Edwin and Morkere, and their king-elect, Edgar. They offered William the crown, and although the duke entered into engagements with them, to their indignation his army continued its devastations. The tactics which William had used in 1063 to get Le Mans served him equally well in England.

That the magnates and the Londoners offered William the throne shows that they were aware that national resistance under a generally-accepted leader was no longer feasible. They were a mixture of cowards and realists. Their common decision was that in the circumstances it was wise to make terms as quickly as possible, especially while they were still in a position to bargain, and turn a conqueror into a legitimate king. William rightly hesitated. He thought that he was tempting fate by taking the shadow of power so soon; he feared that unless his wife was crowned at the same time there might arise an objection to the king-worthiness of his sons; and he may well have read the English motives and felt disinclined to be hampered by even a flimsy bargain. Yet he had already entered into engagements which he was sure to repudiate, like his promise to recognize Archbishop Stigand as his spiritual father. So, with the encouragement of his advisers, who no doubt urged the obvious point that the change of status might discourage rebellion, William overcame his scruples. London was occupied, and on Christmas day in Westminster abbey William was crowned by Archbishop Ealdred of York, and took the usual coronation oath, promising to protect the church, to rule the people with justice, to appoint and keep just laws, and to forbid rapine and all unjust judgments. At the age of thirty-nine William had become an anointed king, and had accepted all the responsibilities of the office. But while he was being crowned, his guards, mistaking the cheers for a riot, set fire to the neighbouring buildings.

Chapter Six

The Conquest of England

ACCORDING to William of Poitiers, who represents informed Norman opinion, the duke had obtained England by Edward's grant of the succession, confirmed by oaths, and by the right of conquest. He had been crowned with the consent, or by the wish, of the English magnates. And his kinship to Edward was close. The two arguments, that William was Edward's legitimate heir and that he was a military conqueror, always sat awkwardly together. Poitiers himself, although his basic theme was the justice of William's claim and that the duke was merely dispossessing an unlawful intruder into his inheritance, found it hard to moderate his exultation over a military conquest and occupation.

This ambivalence is to be found also in William's attitude to his acquisition. After the coronation he did some things like a true king. He confirmed London's customs and ordered the ports and certain roads to be opened to merchants. He is said to have taken various measures for the good of the whole country and of its church; and it is possible that some of the enactments which later were collected as his 'statutes'—such as those granting all men the laws of King Edward and regulating the legal position of the English and French—date back in essentials to this early time. The first of the 'statutes' reads : 'He wished above all things God to be revered throughout his kingdom, the faith of Christ to be preserved inviolate, and peace and security to be kept between the English and Normans.' But if he had thoughts of reforming the English church he put them aside for the moment and decided that the support of the native episcopate was a useful political asset. In any case it was easier to plunder an unreformed church. William is said to have behaved justly himself and also to have demanded that his principal followers should be just, especially as it would have been unwise, as well as unjust, to press the conquered too hard. He condemned all brigandage and seizure of land within the kingdom. He issued strict orders to his knights and soldiers against rape and violence, lechery, and immoderate drinking in taverns, and appointed judges to punish offenders. He was no more indulgent to Normans than to Aquitainians and Bretons.

Poitiers, exasperated by the political events between 1066 and 1071, declaimed in fury that the English were mad not to fall joyfully at William's feet, to love their true and good king. They should discard their prejudices, see his virtues, and recognize that he was greater than all the rulers they had ever had. Cnut the Dane had murdered the noblest of England's sons to assure for himself and his children the English throne. William had not desired even Harold's death but had wanted to enrich and advance him. Moreover he had freed England from that tyrant's rule. The blessings of William's wise government, through which England would become great, would bear testimony against the justice of England's ill-will. So spoke the Normans. But they sadly recognized that there was no popular support for William in the country. The bishops, some of them foreign, were willing to accept the revolution, seeing in it divine retribution for the people's sins. Most of the surviving nobles submitted because no other course seemed open. But, so far as is known, no one went out of his way to welcome the conqueror. The English, the Normans admitted, preferred to have a ruler from their own race.

We can agree that William behaved with moderation. The most striking proof is that he spared Edgar Ætheling, a claimant whom most conquerors would have immediately destroyed. Yet the awkwardness of William's position—as both an heir and a conqueror—must be appreciated. In the winter of 1066–7 he was ruling with the half-hearted co-operation of a few of the natives and had not the physical power to carry out a real and complete conquest. He was riding two uncertain horses and, for the time being, thought that both, although they pulled different ways, gave him better support than either alone. Yet the Normans were naïve if they imagined that the English, after their experiences, were going to welcome their 'deliverer'. To the natives it appeared that 'devils had come through the land with fire and sword and the havoc of war', 'that under the scourges of the chastising God many thousands of the people are thrown down and the kingdom is ravaged by fire and plundering', and 'what can we expect but a miserable end in slaughter unless the infinite and inestimable mercy of the Lord . . . should give us pardon.' The same, or another, contemporary wrote, 'How many thousands of the human race have fallen on evil days ! The sons of kings and earls and nobles . . . are fettered with manacles and chains. . . . How many have lost their limbs by the sword or disease or have been deprived of their eyes, so that when released from prison the common light of the world is a prison for them !' The last of William's 'statutes' reads. 'I forbid that any man be executed or hanged for any offence, but let his eyes be gouged out and his testicles cut off.' Many noblewomen sought refuge in nunneries from the lust of the Normans. In warfare evil things are commonly done and during a military occupation force and justice are often confused. Ecclesiastical penance was imposed on the soldiers for the sins they had committed. But it takes time for the conquered to forget their wrongs.

William only stayed in England for two months after his coronation. He had as much appearance of power as had Edward in 1042–3 and Harold in 1066, that is to say he had been accepted as king by the leading men, had no rival under arms, and had at his disposal the royal demesne. In one way he was stronger than both his predecessors for all the lands of the house of Godwin and of others who had opposed him had escheated to the crown. The earls of Mercia and Northumbria had acknowledged him and were in his power. Formally the whole kingdom was William's and initially he may have been satisfied with the position, for he was accustomed to having lordship over semi-independent counties and honours on his borders—like Ponthieu, the Vexin, Bellême, Maine, and Brittany. It is just possible that if England as a whole had remained quiet, and Earls Edwin and Morkere had found true and justifiable favour with the king, William's rule in England might have been similar to Cnut's. But William differed from his predecessors, including Cnut, by enjoying less popular support and also by quickly turning veiled opposition or indifference into active hostility.

How far William deliberately provoked the English is a very difficult question. It is quite possible to hold one of two extreme views : either that William was a cynical opportunist who offered peace to the English magnates while intending to ruin them at his convenience or that his original benevolent attitude was made impossible by the plots and conspiracies of his English vassals. William was suspected in Normandy of sometimes engineering the destruction of an inconvenient family—as when he secured Mortain for his brother—and he ruined the English bishops in 1070 probably of set purpose, irrespective of their loyalty. But it is likely that in 1067, partly because of the precipitancy of events, he was without a comprehensive plan; and there is much to be said for the purely short-term view that it was the events of 1067 which were decisive.

If so, William reaped the harvest that he himself sowed. His main interest after the coronation seems to have been to secure the royal demesne and the earldoms which had escheated and to accumulate the loot with which to reward his army and make a triumphant return. The earldoms which had fallen in were Harold's (the southern and south-western shires and Herefordshire), Leofwine's (the south-eastern shires), and Gyrth's (East Anglia). Out of these William rewarded, or made first arrangements for, his most important companions. His half-brother, Odo, was placed in Kent, his steward, William fitzOsbern, probably in the Isle of Wight, and Count Brian, the second son of Eudo of Porhoët, count of Penthièvre in Brittany, may have been promised the south-western peninsula. Others of his kinsmen and friends may still have been kept waiting. East Anglia, or perhaps only Norfolk, was entrusted to the Anglo-Breton Ralf de Gael, the son of Ralf the Staller, a servant of King Edward who was still alive. William brought over new troops from France, cavalry and

infantry, and put them in castles and rewarded them with
fiefs, and he made some military expeditions into the
country from the London area. It can be assumed that he
advanced west at least as far as Winchester both for strategic reasons and to seize the royal treasury. But there is
little reason to think that the area of military occupation
extended west of Hampshire or much north of the
Thames. Poitiers claims that no Frenchman was given
anything that was unjustly taken from an Englishman,
and although his view of justice was distinctly partisan,
he may have been technically correct. To defend the occupied area in his absence William appointed two commanders, Odo, bishop of Bayeux, based on Dover Castle,
was to defend the south; William fitzOsbern from Winchester was to watch the north.

William also assembled the spoils. We may be sure that
he had taken Harold's treasure. All sources agree that he
imposed a tax (geld) on the whole country; but, as time
was short and most of the kingdom outside his direct control, he probably took what he could in the way of 'gifts',
and the church may well have suffered most. Poitiers
rhapsodizes over the magnificent treasures which the monasteries willingly bestowed on their new king, the em-
broideries and ornaments, and here his *apologia* for
William is so cynically transparent as to seem insincere.
William also removed from England most of the leaders
as hostages : Archbishop Stigand and some abbots, Edgar
the Ætheling, Earls Edwin, Morkere, and Waltheof (the
son of Siward, once earl of Northumbria), and other
nobles. At Pevensey in February 1067 William paid off
those mercenaries who were returning home and then set
sail in triumph for his own duchy. As Poitiers demonstrates at length, William had done better in every respect
than Julius Caesar.

The new king remained in Normandy until December.
It may have been the happiest time of his life. Bred to
parsimony, he was for a few months lavish. He visited
monasteries to return thanks for his victory and distributed the spoils. To Rome he sent magnificent gifts including, in return for the banner of St Peter, King
Harold's flag, embroidered with an armed man in gold

thread. Many churches in France, Aquitaine, Burgundy, and Auvergne are said to have received gold and jewelled crosses, golden vases and bullion, and embroidered palls. Most no doubt went to the Norman churches, and when William celebrated Easter at Fécamp he held a great court, graced by foreign visitors, at which he dazzled all with his new wealth and state. Yet it was apparently the English captives which aroused the most curiosity. These nobles with their long hair seemed more beautiful than girls.

Wulfstan, bishop of Worcester, a monk born early in the century who was canonized by Pope Innocent III in 1203, was one of those who denounced the effeminate ways of the English on the eve of the Conquest. According to his biographer, Coleman, the bishop, while visiting Northumbria in 1066 with King Harold, urged his master to reform the immorality in the kingdom, an effect, he thought, of peace and affluence. Wulfstan disliked above all the fashion of long hair for men, and to those who refused to get it cut he used to say that men who were ashamed to appear as men and imitated women in the luxuriance of their hair would be no stronger than women in the defence of their country against foreign invaders. And this prophecy, declares Coleman, was proved true, 'for such was the feebleness of the wretched people that after the first battle they never attempted to rise up for liberty behind a common shield; it was as though with Harold had fallen also the whole strength of the country.'

England's disaster was the moralist's opportunity. But those who denounce vice and national degeneracy usually lack historical perspective and a cool judgment. The Vikings were probably long-haired warriors. The Normans themselves soon adopted in England native fashions and were similarly denounced, but seem to have fought none the worse. Much more to the point is that the peace which the kingdom had enjoyed since 1016 had made the English unaccustomed to war, and after Hastings there was simply no leader. Nevertheless, the Norman occupation was to be severely tested between 1066 and 1071 and was occasionally in acute danger. William was prepared for rebellion and appointed as earls and castellans men capable of inspiring terror in the turbulent population.

There has been a tendency among scholars in recent years to treat the Norman Conquest more smoothly than the facts warrant—to regard it as little more than a change in dynasty with a few unpleasant, but temporary, political effects. English resistance has been minimized and the very concept of nationality doubted. In the long view changes can often appear inevitable or trivial. But no one who reads the contemporary narrative accounts will be tempted to take this lofty attitude. For some years after 1066 England was in turmoil. Both the English and the Normans were highly conscious of their race. There were, of course, racial differences in England itself, but these were nothing in comparison with the main cleavage. This is not to say that between 1066 and 1071 there was a patriotic, even a national, war. The mass of the farmers and their labourers were probably little interested in who was king, but they could be provoked if their lands were ravaged or taken over for a castle, or their rents and customs disturbed. The thegns, the nobles, were more emotionally involved, for most had been the vassals of the king or of an earl; but if their new lords stepped neatly into the shoes of the old they were probably not going to repine for long. The abbots and especially the bishops were in a curious situation. Exponents of the insular culture, they were often committed to reform and may sometimes have expected it from the Normans. The foreigners among the episcopate may have welcomed the change, and all by their training were prepared to submit to the powers of the world, whoever they might be. As for the earls and greatest nobles they were either dead or had lost their prestige. As a result of this situation there could be no united struggle against the occupying forces. But there was bound to be resistance and local rebellion whenever the new rule was too rough; those held in honourable captivity were sure to conspire; and the dispossessed and discontented inevitably looked for outside help.

The ravaging after Hastings and the gathering of spoils might soon have been accepted as the inevitable consequences of war had not William abandoned his kingdom so quickly and for so long. He lingered in Normandy for more than nine months and would probably have stayed at least over winter—a full year—had he not been alarmed by news from England. This long absence is surely the key to William's attitude at the time. He was not required in Normandy. The duchy had been peaceful and was in no danger. William was, therefore, treating England exactly as he treated Maine—a possession which, once acquired, only demanded his presence when there was trouble. It is difficult to avoid the conclusion that had England remained at peace and paid contentedly all the royal revenues it would have seen little of its king. It is also hard not to believe that William was deceived by the ease of his initial success in England. In any case, by removing the terror of his presence and entrusting the government to subordinates he provoked a situation which required his continuous presence for over four years and completely transformed the nature of the Conquest.

According to Orderic Vital, who here is glossing William of Poitiers, William's deputies, Odo and William fitzOsbern, and their armies disregarded the king's orders and behaved badly during his absence. The castellans oppressed rich and poor with unjust exactions and insults. The commanders acted too savagely and refused to hear and judge equitably the complaints of the oppressed; they not only protected the soldiers who were looting and raping but also punished those victims who were foolish enough to complain. The men of Kent, by repute the least savage of the natives, were provoked to invite Eustace of Boulogne to come and save them from Odo. The count, who had quarrelled with William, presumably over his reward, tried to take Dover; but his expedition, although well supported by the English, was a fiasco. William was compelled to return on 6 December 1067, and brought reinforcements, including Roger of Montgomery. By flattery and fair words, and by his very presence, he calmed some of the indignation. His wife, now carrying the future King Henry I, joined him before Whitsun 1068 when she was crowned queen at Westminster by Archbishop Ealdred. Matilda stayed until she had given birth to her son and then, in the next year, went home again.

If we have understood William's attitude aright his sole intention in 1068 was to restore the situation in England which had overstrained his deputies, and by some military progresses to overawe the whole kingdom. What he may not have realized was that, in the absence of a generally accepted or popular king, English political unity, still fragile, had simply broken up and that the various outlying provinces and districts were falling into anarchy. The south-west peninsula, once part of Harold's earldom, was sheltering the women of his family and his illegitimate sons, but no eminent or possible leader, and seems to have been waiting sullenly for the future to unfold. East Anglia was probably satisfactorily controlled by its bishop, Æthelmaer, Stigand's brother, and Ralf the Staller and Ralf de Gael. Mercia was deprived of its earl, and, at least in West Mercia, William seems to have relied principally on Æthelwig, abbot of Evesham, and also on Wulfstan, bishop of Worcester. The Welsh marches were in a sorry state. It is unlikely that William fitzOsbern could find much time for Hereford; we hear nothing of the bishop; and we know that a Worcester thegn, Eadric the Wild, was waging a private war against Richard fitzScrob and other Normans who had been planted in Herefordshire in Edward's reign, and was able to call on the ready help of Welsh princes.

Northumbria was a special case. Still conscious of its independent history and remembering the Norwegian kings of York, aware that it had successfully expelled Earl Tostig in 1065, different in racial make-up and social organization from the rest of the kingdom, it had fallen away completely. That Earl Morkere and some of the Northumbrian nobles were in William's hands counted for little. Morkere had no roots in the province; there were many descendants of former earls available; and the land was full of courageous nobles who were willing to fight. Moreover the Northumbrians could call on two outside powers for help—the king of Scots and the king of Denmark. The former would gladly extend his kingdom to the Humber and the latter had a claim to Edward's throne; and both were less foreign than William. Against this hostility William had only the influence of Archbishop

Ealdred of York, a bishop who had spent most of his life in the south of England, and the courage of a few adventurers, both Northumbrian and alien, who offered to intervene in William's interest. Copsig, once Earl Tostig's deputy in Northumbria, had joined William, found favour, and had been entrusted with the administration of the north. In March 1067, or possibly 1068, he was murdered.

Such a situation, however, was not daunting to an eleventh-century prince. Æthelred had ruled England in rather similar conditions. William had known worse in Normandy. The English had no agreed purpose and no acknowledged leader and had no castles. The only fortresses were the walled cities and boroughs. William had a secure base in England, a professional army, and moreover an implacable determination to destroy all opposition. The fighting which started in 1068 lasted without much respite into 1071. The English nobles deserted William one by one and different areas rebelled in turn. It was this dispersion and fitfulness of the revolts which made William's task possible. As the tide of rebellion rose the king had several armies in the field—his own and those of some of his most trusted kinsmen and friends, principally Odo of Bayeux, William fitzOsbern, and Brian of Brittany. These commanders had some of their own household troops and vassals with them, but for the rank and file relied on hired soldiers. Owing to the length of the campaign and the unpleasant conditions the armies were hard to keep together and there seems to have been a fairly rapid turnover. There was also the problem of dispersal of strength, for as the war developed William studded England with castles and each required an isolated garrison. Whenever possible William called up for military service the English who owed the duty, and against some rebels, especially in the south, they proved most useful. But to pay for the war William had to tax the country heavily and also take loot; and these financial exactions increased the unrest.

William began the year 1068 by subduing the south-west. Exeter had refused demands to submit and was, apparently, organizing a league of boroughs for self-defence. When William arrived with his army there were divided counsels in the city. The leading men offered to surrender and gave hostages, but the mass of the people disavowed their actions and closed the gates. William had one of the hostages blinded before the town and after an eighteen-day siege, during which he attempted to undermine the walls, the city capitulated on terms. William permitted no looting or atrocities and imposed no penalty. His sole demand was the construction of a castle within the city and its garrisoning. He then perambulated Cornwall before returning to Winchester for Easter. Harold's family was forced into exile and only the sons attempted later to return.

By the summer Mercia and Northumbria were in revolt. Earls Edwin and Morkere abandoned William and joined the Welsh; but when the king built a castle at Warwick, which he entrusted to Henry of Beaumont, the earls submitted and were pardoned. More serious for William, Edgar the Ætheling, his mother, and his two sisters fled to Scotland and were received by King Malcolm Canmore, who married Margaret, possibly in 1069. The Northumbrians seized York and William marched against them. He fortified Nottingham, giving the castle to William Peverel, and then entered York where also he built a castle. The bishop of Durham, Æthelwine, surrendered, acted as intermediary with the king of Scots, and prevented his intervention. William gave the county of Durham now, or a little later, to Robert of Comines, a Flemish knight, and returned south, building castles at Lincoln, Huntingdon, and Cambridge on the way. In the meantime Harold's sons, who had taken refuge in Ireland, attacked Bristol and Somerset. They were, however, treated merely as pirates by the English and were fought off by native troops. The events of this year caused some of the Normans to lose heart. According to Orderic Vital the wives whom the soldiers had left behind in Normandy, and who feared to join them in England, were demanding their husbands' return. It was a situation unsatisfactory for the English and Norman women alike. William offered the mutinous soldiers rich fiefs, and even larger ones when the whole of England was subdued, and his loyal companions appealed to their honour; but there were serious defections from the army, including, it is said, Hugh of Grandmesnil who had fought at Hastings and been in command of the Winchester area. William had to recruit more mercenary soldiers and with promise of greater rewards.

The year 1069 opened with the murder of Robert of Comines and his men at Durham, and of Robert fitz-Richard, a castellan at York. Then Edgar came down from Scotland, rallied the Northumbrian leaders, was received in York, and attacked the royal castles. William Malet, the local commander, was in great danger; but before Easter William drove Edgar out again, sacked the city and left the trusted William fitzOsbern as his lieutenant. In the summer Harold's sons invaded North Devon, perhaps with a larger fleet than before, only to be overwhelmed by Count Brian. A series of local uprisings in the west also harassed the Normans. The men of Dorset and Somerset attacked Robert of Mortain's castle at Montacute but were quelled by Geoffrey bishop of Coutances. The men of Chester and the Welsh attacked Shrewsbury and were aided by the burgesses, the men of Shropshire, and Eadric the Wild. Exeter, again defended by its citizens, was attacked by insurgents from Devon and Cornwall. The king sent his commanders from the north and southwest, William fitzOsbern and Count Brian, against these insurrections. Shrewsbury they found burned out and abandoned by the enemy, but at Exeter they inflicted heavy losses on the attackers.

In the autumn a new pretender intervened, Svein Estrithson, king of Denmark. Svein, the son of Cnut's sister and the cousin of the late King Harold and Queen Edith, Edward's widow, was another who claimed that Edward had bequeathed him the throne. Slower to move than William, he had now prepared an expeditionary force, with auxiliaries from Poland, Frisia, Saxony, and even *Leuticia* (possibly Lausitz), carried, it was said, by up to 300 ships, under the command of his brother, Osbern, a prince who had been expelled from England in 1049, and two of his sons. Bishops were with the army, and it was an expedition perhaps smaller than, but certainly comparable with, William's three years before. The invaders coasted and ravaged from Dover to the Humber where they were joined by Edgar and other English nobles. The combined forces took the castles at York and massacred or captured the garrison (including William Malet), while the city burned again. During the hostilities the old archbishop, Ealdred, died. The England he had known was in ruins. As the king once more marched north the Danes took refuge in the Humber and the English leaders once more retreated. Unlike the invaders in 1066 —Harold Hardrada and Tostig and then William—Osbern and Edgar feared a decisive encounter. The possessor could often afford to decline a pitched battle, but the claimant seldom. The indecision, perhaps cowardice, of the allies was a tribute to William's military reputation and a sign that, if he did not falter, he was going to win through.

Since the Danes lurked in the rivers which flowed into the Humber the king could not reach them. His answer was systematically to ravage the land and thus deny them provisions and also discourage their English friends. He entered Lindsey and, detaching his brother, Robert of Mortain, and Robert count of Eu to watch the enemy, made for York. Rebels held him up for three weeks at the crossing of the River Aire at Pontefract, but eventually he got through to York. He decided to stay and destroy the north once and for all. He had the coronation regalia brought up from Winchester for the Christmas feast, and then carried out a winter campaign in the roughest country and harshest weather. In January 1070 he rode north to the Tees, devastating the countryside, and Earl Waltheof and Gospatric, two of the most important English leaders, submitted to him. He then pushed up to Hexham on the Tyne before returning to York. Unrelenting he decided to attack Chester and the Welsh. He crossed the Pennines in the middle of winter, often on foot, while the mercenaries from Brittany, Anjou, and Maine mutinied and deserted, complaining that he was imposing intolerable duties on them. But William reached Chester, where he built a castle, and devastated Mercia. He had promised the victors a rest after their labours and pointed out that rewards could only be won by hard work. When William reached Salisbury before Easter he gave the loyal soldiers their pay with thanks and ordered that the mutinous and deserters should be kept under arms for a further forty days as punishment. The king believed that the backbone of the resistance in England had been broken by his exertions. Northumbria was left ruined and suffered the inevitable famine and pestilence. The Danish fleet was discouraged and the English rebels were losing all heart. In 1070 Eadric the Wild submitted. It is recorded that in February William plundered all the monasteries in England. Rents and taxes must have been difficult to collect and the king's expenses were considerable.

The crisis in the struggle was indeed past, but the war was by no means over. In the spring of 1070 King Svein joined his fleet in the Humber and decided to raid East Anglia. This area had hitherto remained quiet, but at Easter William had had Archbishop Stigand and Bishop Æthelmaer, perhaps the greatest landholders in the province, deposed. The Danes were again welcomed by the people, and Svein dispatched his brother with an army to Ely. Hereward the Wake, a thegn of Peterborough Abbey, looted that church in order to prevent the treasures passing into the hands of a Norman abbot, and carried the spoils to Ely. By now Svein was probably as convinced as his brother that William was too strongly entrenched to be pushed out, and plunder became his only aim. William offered him free passage home with the Peterborough treasure, and Svein sailed, only to be caught in the autumn gales and see his fleet dispersed and much of the plunder lost.

Hereward remained in possession of Ely; and in 1071 the Earls Edwin and Morkere completed the ruin of their ineffectual lives by fleeing from William's court when all hope of a successful rebellion was gone. On any reading of the events between 1066 and 1072 the conduct of these earls must appear mischievous. By their ancestry and position the natural leaders of the laity after the destruction of the house of Godwin, they gave an example neither of courageous and steadfast military opposition nor of honourable and complete surrender, and so must bear much responsibility for the sad plight of their earldoms and of the whole country. In 1071 they probably intended to escape to Scotland. Morkere, however, turned away to Ely and Edwin was killed by one of his own men. Bishop Æthelwine of Durham had also gone from Peterborough to Ely, and the island in the Fens had become the last refuge of the English rebels and outlaws. William invested the place by land and sea and captured Æthelwine and Morkere and many others. The leaders were put in prison, the lesser men mutilated and allowed to go free. Hereward and his band were not among these. The outlaw broke out, and escaped into legend.

William had at last subdued the kingdom of England. In 1072 he mounted a military and naval expedition against Scotland. It is interesting to note that Eadric the Wild served in the army. When the king reached Abernethy on the Tay, Malcolm submitted, became William's vassal, and gave hostages. Edgar Ætheling was forced to leave Scotland for Flanders. Hastings, a tiny battle, is always remembered. The six years' warfare which followed is sometimes not given its proper importance. If Hastings shows William's decisiveness and audacity, the subsequent campaigns prove that he possessed the highest abilities of a military commander : resolution, coolness, patience, a flair for marching on the centres of trouble, courage in risking deep penetration of disturbed areas, and, above all, the power to drive his own troops up to, and beyond, the limits of their endurance. William's political ability is almost impossible to judge from these events because we cannot be certain of his policy. If he was sure that the English magnates were insincere in their subjection and deliberately played cat and mouse with them, he won at great cost a hazardous game. But if he merely wanted to rule like his predecessors in England, then his political skill must be faulted because his government was too rough for the purpose. By 1072 William had conquered the kingdom. Such an internal conquest had been achieved before by the son and grandsons of King Alfred, and for a time had greatly strengthened royal power. That it had now been repeated, even more thoroughly, by a Norman duke and at the price of great slaughter and widespread destruction, was even more momentous for the kingdom.

Chapter Seven

William's Followers in England

WILLIAM'S conquest of Maine was not followed by a Norman settlement of the county and his claim to the overlordship of Brittany was innocent of any idea of obtaining land. Similarly if William had stepped peacefully into King Edward's shoes all that he would have obtained, at least at first, was the royal demesne; and before 1066 he negotiated with the English earls on that understanding. But owing to the way in which he obtained the throne the earldoms and estates of Harold and his kin and the estates of others who had opposed him were forfeit and by 1072 most other large estate-holders had been destroyed. William and his friends knew in 1066 that if they defeated Harold there would be land as spoils, but that they would demolish almost completely the top-structure of landlordship in England was probably beyond their dreams.

The position in England was that the king, the church, and the nobles had estates which consisted largely in rents paid by reeves, 'farmers', or lessees. These estate managers or speculators collected the lord's rents and customs due from the towns, villages, and other agricultural groupings, units often called manors by the Normans, and made a profit on the transaction. The lord had in addition under-tenants, vassals, who rendered him services, and sometimes a rent instead or as well, for the estates. The individual contracts between a lord and his under-tenants, lessees, farmers, and reeves varied considerably in detail, but their purpose was to provide him with a revenue and useful services. This superstructure disappeared with the English aristocracy, and was replaced by new enfeoffments made by the king. There is no evidence that Norman peasants crossed the Channel, and the Norman settlement in England must be seen as similar to that in Apulia and Sicily or to the later English plantation in Ireland—the establishment of foreign land-lords over an indigenous population.

William reserved for himself a large demesne, perhaps a fifth of the cultivated area of England. Domesday Book, which surveys England south of the Rivers Ribble and Tees, lists *terra regis* in every shire except Shropshire and Chester. Thus William re-endowed the English monarchy and restored a position which had been eroded since the days of Edgar. In the Middle Ages royal estates normally ran down owing to the claims of gratitude on each new king, and were replenished only by a change of dynasty (which added the new family's private estates) or by in-ternal 'conquests'—the destruction of great landholders by some ruthless king. William made himself and the monarchy rich. The number of his men to whom he gave large estates is quite small. Essentially he rewarded his old friends and those who in some important capacity had furthered the conquest—his half-brothers, some favourite and trusted Norman vassals, like Geoffrey, bishop of Cou-tances, William fitzOsbern, Roger of Montgomery, Wil-liam of Warenne, Hugh of Avranches, and Richard fitz-Gilbert, and some social equals, most of whom were re-lated to him, like Counts Alan the Red and Brian of Brittany, Eustace of Boulogne, Robert of Eu, and William of Évreux. And in general William continued to use these men as his captains in his various wars. There was also a crowd of smaller men whom William enfeoffed, the sub-ordinate military commanders, the castellans, some soldiers, especially the technical men, crossbowmen and engineers, and the personal servants, stewards, dispensers, cooks, doctors, barbers, foresters, huntsmen, carpenters, and so on. For the king and his major beneficiaries there was a fairly long list of dependants to reward; but it was not unmanageable and the claims could easily be met.

The main enfeoffments were made gradually within the period 1066–72. Owing to the lack of statistics and also to the opportunist element William could not have had a master plan; but nevertheless he broke the English and substituted a Norman pattern. In place of the great provincial earldoms he created smaller marcher counties. The ring round Normandy of Ponthieu, Aumale, the Vexin, Évreux, Bellême, and Mortain was repeated in England with Kent, Cornwall, Hereford, Shrewsbury, Chester, Northumberland, Richmond, and Norfolk. William created these positions for his most faithful men. In the first phase Odo of Bayeux had Kent, Count Brian of Brittany Cornwall, William fitzOsbern the Isle of Wight and Hereford. About 1071 Roger of Montgomery, who held the castle of Arundel and the town of Chichester, was made earl of Shrewsbury. Early in 1070 Gherbod, a Fleming, who had obtained a large part of Mercia and the city of Chester, was recognized as earl; but he abandoned this troublesome acquisition and was replaced in 1071 as earl of Chester by a Norman baron, Hugh of Avranches. Richmond by 1086 was in the possession of Alan the Red, a count of Brittany, the brother of Brian, who was succeeded by two other brothers in turn; and the son of the last of these was created an earl before 1136. Northumberland and Norfolk, as attenuated successors to Northumbria and East Anglia, were left in native hands. The Anglo-Breton Ralf de Gael replaced Gyrth in Norfolk. After various experiments beyond the Humber, Waltheof, earl of Huntingdon and Northampton, the son of Cnut's Earl Siward, was appointed earl of Northumberland in 1072 and married to William's niece, Judith. These two earls, and probably Brian of Cornwall, were broken in 1075. Norfolk was apparently left vacant, but in Northumbria, because of the unrest and the danger from Scotland, William had to go on trying. First he appointed the new bishop of Durham, Walcher, a Lotharingian, to the office. When Walcher was murdered in 1080 Aubrey, a Norman knight, was allowed to try his hand. When he quickly gave up, Robert of Mowbray, the nephew of the bishop of Coutances, succeeded where the others had failed.

William deliberately contrived local concentrations of land for the holders of the new marcher honours. Their earl or lord was usually the major landholder in the shire, sometimes almost the sole tenant-in-chief. Elsewhere William normally granted the lands of one or more English predecessors to the new beneficiary—and the marcher lords often had estates of that sort in other parts of the kingdom as well. The result of this method of distribution was dispersed lordships on the usual contemporary pattern, an arrangement which was sometimes found inconvenient, and ameliorated, but never destroyed, by exchange or sub-infeudation.

If we turn to Domesday Book, which lists the tenants-in-chief in each shire—those who held their fiefs directly of the king—we can count about 300 laymen. These are the men whom William had rewarded before 1086. Only a very select group held vast estates. The basic division is between those who were given a nobleman's estate and the rest. Just over a hundred of these fiefs were later recognized as baronies, and their holders as the king's barons. The others were deemed to be held of the king by less honourable tenures.

Each of William's barons had his own kinsmen, friends, and followers to reward, and some of these dependants accumulated large mesne estates and were also lords of men. We are given in Domesday Book, shire by shire, the names of the tenants-in-chief and of their immediate vassals. It may well be that the names of most foreigners who obtained a grant of land are recorded. But it is extremely difficult to count the under-tenants because many had common names, undifferentiated by a surname; and so one man, who held of several lords within a single shire and also of the same or other lords in several shires, can easily be counted several times over.

To get some idea of the pattern of local settlement we can glance at a shire. Devonshire will serve; it is large; it had quickly submitted and had not been devastated; and, as it had formed part of Harold's earldom, all the large estates had changed hands without, so far as can be seen, disturbing the substructure. In this shire 53 tenants-in-chief are listed. Less than half of these were barons, the others being ecclesiastical tenants, thegns, and serjeants. Eight of the most important barons, for example Hugh of Avranches, earl of Chester, his future brother-in-law, William of Eu, the second son of Robert, count of Eu, and Richard fitzGilbert (count of Brionne), lord of Clare (Suffolk), had only small holdings in Devon. Others, although they had sizable estates in the county, were not primarily Devon barons, for example Geoffrey of Mowbray, bishop of Coutances, Robert, count of Mortain, William of Falaise, and Walter of Douai. Only a few had their main estates in Devon. Among these were Baldwin fitzGilbert, sheriff of Devon and brother of Richard fitz-Gilbert, William Capra, Robert of Aumale, and the Breton, Juhel of Totnes. There were in fact in the county no more than fifteen men of both national and local importance, and only two of these, Geoffrey of Coutances and Robert of Mortain, were barons of the highest rank. Most would have been absentees; and it is likely that the sheriff, or *vicomte*, Baldwin, a relative of the king, had the greatest local weight and impact.

The number of foreign under-tenants on these baronial estates is about 140, and there is certainly some duplication here. The pattern of enfeoffment varied considerably. Some great men, like Earl Hugh, had given none of their small Devon holdings away. The bishop of Coutances and the count of Mortain had each put in one large mesne tenant and a number of small ones, 9 and 14 respectively. The sheriff Baldwin had distributed fiefs fairly evenly among 24 vassals. We also notice that on almost all estates some Englishmen, either persisting from Edward's reign or more recently introduced, were present as mesne tenants.

To estimate from the evidence of Domesday Book the total number of foreigners who settled in England between 1066 and 1086 is an extremely hazardous operation. The number of foreigners enfeoffed with English land may have been about 1,500. The total influx may, therefore, have been in the region of five to ten thousand men and women. If these figures appear low it must be remembered that the settlers, apart from the foreign clergy, burgesses, and merchants, were essentially men of honourable birth, mainly nobles, who brought some vassals, retainers, and servants with them. The total population of the country has been estimated at between one and two million. The conquest must temporarily have reduced the number. The new settlers cannot have compensated for the English losses through battle, famine, and disease.

The king had distributed territorial largesse to his men, and they to theirs. What each granted was the profitability of the estates—the entitlement to the rents, services, and jurisdiction which the previous lords had enjoyed. The traditional value was the sum of what the reeves, lessees, and 'farmers', had customarily paid to the lord's steward (the *valuit* of Domesday Book). Owing to the ravaging in 1065–71 dues could not always be collected in full and so the actual value (the *valet* of the survey) could be something less. On the other hand, a rack-renting, or even a progressive, landlord could often push up the value in a short time. When we consider in what circumstances the estates were granted we must accept that the distribution was something of a lottery. Orderic Vital, because of his Anglo-Norman blood torn in his attitude, observed, when listing some of the greatest beneficiaries, that William had created tribunes and centurions out of the meanest Norman soldiers; and, when the chronicler dramatized the events of 1075, he put bitter words into the mouths of the rebel earls : William had not honoured properly those who had made the conquest possible; he had ungratefully defrauded those who had spilled their blood in his service; to the wounded veterans he had given farms which were both infertile and devastated by war, and, after they had restocked them, sometimes even taken them away again. The charges are inconsistent, but revealing. There must have been some envy and complaint among those who believed that they were entitled to a reward.

These tensions were on the surface. The economic substructure was relatively stable. There is no evidence that the new lords made drastic changes. At first there were many arbitrary actions : tenants evicted to provide fiefs for newcomers or to allow a hall or castle to be built, encroachments on other estates, the misunderstanding of Old-English tenures, the many carelessnesses and roughnesses of men who were strangers, uncertain of their rights, and often contemptuous of the natives. But, once established, the new landholders had no great reason to disturb the arrangements they inherited. They were richer than ever before; all those with large estates were for the most part absentees; and in the early days they probably lacked the interest, time, and knowledge to interfere. Any one of them could have demanded labour for building a castle or hall or required higher rents from the 'farmers' and reeves. But only the most determined and ruthless would have persisted if told that the lands could not produce more or faced with the passive resistance of the inhabitants of the villages. After the disturbances the village communities, with their priest and reeve, and the hamlets continued to live much as before, observing the same customs. William, possibly under Norman ecclesiastical influence, disliked chattel slavery, and after the Conquest the status of slave began to disappear from the manors. But in 1086 slaves were still plentiful in England.

In this lower stratum of the kingdom's economy there was massive continuity. But at the landlord level there was, as we have seen, considerable change. It has been calculated from the Domesday survey that in 1086 about a fifth of the land was royal demesne, a quarter held by the church, and half in the hands of the greater lay tenants-in-chief of the king. There was also much displacement of Englishmen in the landlord class immediately below this highest category. It is inconceivable that this rapid and extensive replacement of an Anglo-Danish by a French aristocracy should not have produced social, legal, and economic changes. But, owing to the absence of clear information, the subject remains controversial and obscure.

It can safely be assumed that the new grantors, mainly the king and his barons, gave estates as lords to vassals to be held as fiefs, the vassal doing homage and swearing fealty, and also performing services in return for the grant. We need not concern ourselves minutely with the problem of continuity from Anglo-Saxon England. It is clear, on the evidence of Domesday Book, that Old-English tenures could usually be described without difficulty in Norman feudal terms and it is obvious that the new pattern fitted fairly easily over the old. We can also be confident that the grantors, especially the king, expected to receive in return for the enfeoffment all those rents, customs, and services which had traditionally been rendered from the estates. William was abrogating no rights which he had inherited from Edward. The Domesday survey supports this view. It records the customs of the boroughs and shires and the hidage (the rateable value which determined the liability to geld and military service) of the estates. It is a record of ancient duties and gives no indication that the Normans had introduced great change.

We must, however, believe that Domesday Book does not tell the whole story. The commissioners were not asked to investigate the personal duties of vassals to lords. And it is in regard to this unrecorded aspect of tenure that historians are uncertain. Edward's earls and thegns had owed him loyalty and faithfulness, service in his army and attendance at his court, and some payments, such as heriot, or death-duty. Whether these duties were based on their rank or their lands mattered little then and can hardly matter much to us. The obligations of William's vassals in the duchy seem to have been similar. And it would be unreasonable to think that the transplantation of some of these men to England could have led either to fundamental changes in Norman habit or to a complete break with English traditions. Two similar social conventions existed for a time (1066–71) side by side, and, as Frenchmen displaced the conquered, Norman customs prevailed. The relationship between a Norman lord and his Norman vassals in England was bound to be moulded according to Norman ideas (and similarly for the Bretons, Flemish and other nationalities in England); but the new customs differed probably only in detail from Old-English usage. Moreover, in William's reign we should be prepared to find a French façade covering, and not much more than concealing, English structures.

Because traditional obligations between lord and vassal were assumed in England, no written record was made of the terms on which the new enfeoffments were made. Indeed, since the duties of the king's barons became a matter of dispute in the twelfth century and were hotly debated in the thirteenth, it seems unlikely that when William granted an honour to a baron, or a baron to one of his men, any detailed conditions were imposed. The customs were regarded as too familiar to need expression and too miscellaneous to make definition possible.

It has, however, usually been held since the imaginative studies of J. H. Round that in one respect William did break arbitrarily with the past, and also state a precise duty, when granting land to his barons—that he fixed the military service of his vassals by allocating them a quota of knights to be furnished to the royal army, a quota which bore no relationship at all to the Old-English liabilities. Yet this remains far from clear. If William did indeed impose quotas of troops similar to those he is believed to have exacted from some Norman bishops and barons, neither the king nor his vassals kept a record of the obligation. In 1166 Henry II asked his English barons some questions about the number of knights they and their ancestors had enfeoffed both before 1135 and after, and how many they were retaining, apparently with scutage or taxation in mind. The barons were often in doubt about the answers and the figures returned seem arbitrary. In any case the relevance of these figures, and their total of some 5,000, to William I's reign is uncertain, especially as in the later period, for which we have records, the assessments were often modified. Moreover, there appears to be little connexion between this twelfth-century *servitium debitum* and William's armies as they are described by contemporaries. Whenever an eleventh-century royal or baronial army is seen in action its composition is miscellaneous: barons, thegns, knights, mercenaries, and auxiliaries, and usually men of several nationalities. English troops (as opposed to Norman) are mentioned whether rebellions are being suppressed in the kingdom or William is fighting in Maine or at Gerberoy. Bishop Walcher's second-in-command as earl of Northumbria, his kinsman Gilbert, had at least two English thegns in the troop he took to escort the bishop to a dangerous meeting at Gateshead. To make a theoretical distinction, as some historians do, between the feudal host (foreign knights) and the 'national' *fyrd* (English thegns—some would add ceorls) is not only perverse, for the distinction was obviously not made at the time, but also useless, because it hides realities.

As we do not know whether William in fact specified the number of soldiers that each baron had to produce for the royal army, or, if he did, what the figures were, the subject does not invite dogmatic theories. We may, however, suggest that in William's reign the Old-English liability remained. This, as we know, for it is described several times in Domesday Book—and must therefore have been of interest in 1086—was based on the hidage, normally one soldier from each five hides. It is common sense to expect that when an English baron was called upon to put down an uprising or join the king with his troops, he would summon to his standard all soldiers in his barony who owed the duty; and these would surely include those Englishmen who would have answered the summons of the baron's predecessor or of Edward's earl or sheriff. In the present state of our knowledge we can say no more than that William, always in need of soldiers, required his barons when necessary to raise all the forces they could. After the years of crisis other arrangements may have been made. No Norman or later king cared for the miscellaneous troops provided by their barons. They much preferred select quotas of professional knights and money with which to hire suitable mercenaries.

We should carefully observe the military crisis of 1085–6 when a Danish invasion was threatened and there was near panic in England. William was on the Continent and had probably drained England of all troops over and above the needs of the garrison. On Lanfranc's advice the king recruited mercenaries in France and Brittany, brought them over, and distributed them among the various baronial courts. We get a glimpse of the bishop of Worcester's share eating their heads off and drinking themselves silly in the priory until Wulfstan was moved to close the buttery. At whose cost these quotas were maintained we are not told, but it was William who paid many of the soldiers off as soon as the campaigning season ended. At Christmas he ordered the 'Domesday' survey to be made. Orderic Vital writes, 'He made a survey of the military strength of the kingdom of England, and he discovered 60,000 soldiers, whom he ordered to be made ready whenever necessity demanded.' Orderic, having lived his first ten years in England close to the household of Earl Roger of Montgomery, one of William's principal military commanders, had in September 1085 been sent

as an oblate to St Évroult in Normandy. The future historian may have got it all wrong; but he, or his informants,
believed that a territorial survey disclosed the liability to
military service in 1086, and that to discover the hidage
was to establish the service.

Although it has been claimed that feudalism is society
organized for war, in fact we know little of the details of
eleventh-century military service. By the age of records,
the twelfth century, the English feudal army was obsolescent and its customs are poor evidence for earlier practice.
We have some information about castle-guard—the
garrisoning of royal and baronial castles; but important
features, such as the length of service owed to the royal
army in each year and the area within which barons were
obliged to serve, remain unknown. They were probably
not defined. Later the barons maintained that the period
of service should be limited to forty days. This period
occurs frequently in feudal custom and it may have been
the customary term for hiring a soldier. Certainly in 1070
William retained his mutinous troops for a further forty
days. It was, we should note, a convenient accounting
period. If a soldier's daily pay was 3*d*. his total reward
would be ten shillings, if 4*d*. one mark of silver, and if 6*d*.
one pound. It is possible that in considering the military
aspect of feudalism too much emphasis has usually been
placed on the vassal-knight and too little on the hired
mercenary.

Besides the duty of serving with their men in the king's
army the barons seem to have had all the other contemporary feudal duties, such as attending the king's court
and taking their disputes there, supporting him loyally
against all men, giving him aid and counsel when asked,
consulting him about marriage alliances, the alienation
of land, the founding of monasteries, and other important
matters. The king had the right to make the heir to a
barony pay a sum of money for permission to succeed
(relief) and he claimed the wardship and marriage of the
heir if under age. William's barons, although predominantly Norman, came also from Brittany, Flanders, and
other French lands, and had not all the same traditions.
But gradually over the years, as a result of disputes, a body

of custom was evolved and the duties were defined which are sometimes called 'the feudal incidents'.

The lesser men enfeoffed by William usually owed him their professional services in return. In other words, William rewarded some of his knights and servants for their services and they and their descendants retained those duties. The office of doorkeeper, captain of the king's ship, and so on, had been enfeoffed. Such men were later termed serjeants, and their fiefs serjeanties.

The barons organized their baronies on the model of the king and the kingdom. They too had their barons (honorial barons), knights, and serjeants and their courts. They too enfeoffed their men on terms for which we lack the details; and in each barony or honour, as in the kingdom, the feudal law had to be worked out. In general it may be thought that each baron had over his own men rights similar to those which the king had over his barons, but with two important exceptions. William did not allow (except on the Welsh march) the right of private war in England, and he insisted that baronial troops should fight only in the king's army. Probably in England, as often in Normandy, household and enfeoffed knights were mostly used by barons for escort and messenger duties and for garrison service in castles. In the absence of a postal service and other mechanical means of communication messenger duties were heavy. We know that Gilbert, count of Brionne, frequently sent his knight, Herlwin, the founder of Bec, on missions to other courts; and when Herlwin refused to carry a message which he considered morally indefensible to Duke Robert, Gilbert deprived him of his fief. The other qualitative difference between the barony and the kingdom was that whereas the king had no superior lord to keep him in order, William's hand was heavy on his barons. The vassals of a baron could appeal to the king's court against denial of justice or wrongful action; and there is evidence that the Norman barons in England thought that William interfered far too much. Typical of his attitude is that in 1086 at Salisbury, before he left England probably never to see it again, he compelled all important landholders in England, irrespective of their tenure and status, to swear fealty to him. William intended to be a king as well as a feudal lord, and even as feudal lord was prepared to disregard custom and in special circumstances establish direct relations with important rear-vassals. All the Normans felt insecure in England and most for a time were willing to accept the unusually close bonds. They were in military occupation of the country and still amenable to discipline.

The situation created by the royal and baronial enfeoffments after 1066 has been described as the introduction of the feudal system into England. This view has become unpopular for two main reasons. There are historians who dislike the terminology and there are those who dispute the facts. Although 'system' is a respectable, indeed basic, sociological term, it is apt to be misunderstood by those not trained in that discipline and give a false impression of rigidity and regular pattern. Historians deal more with the particular than with generalizations and, since the societies conventionally described as feudal both underwent with the years considerable change and also differed widely from each other at any one time, there is a tendency for each historian to define feudalism in his own local terms. This only encourages meaningless controversy. Such controversies have been particularly associated with the Norman conquest of England, for by the end of the nineteenth century it was believed that pre-Conquest England was in its social organization fundamentally different from contemporary France and that Normandy was feudal and England was not. Since then these judgments have been modified. There are historians who consider that the Old-English kingdom was by the eleventh century at least partly or basically feudal and it has become increasingly doubtful whether at that time Normandy was as 'perfectly feudal' as is often believed. Hence we can, if we choose, put both societies within a feudal system, as understood by the sociologists, and discuss their differences without terminological disputes.

The minor differences between Old-English and Norman feudalism are not, however, our concern in this context. The major change was that since the new enfeoffments were made in a very short span of time they were governed by the same ideas. This feature produced a social class unnaturally uniform in structure. In Domesday Book English landholding is described exclusively in terms of the fief. All estates were, or were soon to be, fiefs, and every piece of land was held by someone from someone else in a chain which sooner or later reached the king. But the application of common principles did not produce a simple pattern; and those who study the actual tenurial details are, because of the complexity they find, inclined to speak jokingly of 'the feudal jungle' in England. Most important barons held parcels of land of each other and even of their own or another's mesne tenant. Some small tenants-in-chief held large mesne estates from various lords. Every possible tenurial complication existed in England within two decades of the Conquest. It was a complex chain, rather than a ladder with rungs, which tied all men ultimately to the king, and the pattern has none of the orderliness of a pyramid to which it is sometimes likened.

As a result of the new enfeoffments there were in William's reign two main nations in England, the French and the English. The cleavage between the foreign lords and the indigenous population was real, although hardly in itself of much significance. There always was a cleavage between the nobles and the agrarian population. Of great importance for the future was the persistence, scattered among the larger fiefs, of a very considerable number of English smaller landholders, men in the strata between the barons and the working farmers. It was at this level that intermarriage could soon take place; such men quickly became bi-lingual; and a class of country gentlemen formed which achieved a synthesis of the two cultures. There was also a modest influx of foreign traders and artificers into England after 1066. Sometimes they established a community within or without an old borough, occasionally they settled by a new centre, often a castle. But this was a relatively minor effect of the Conquest. England and Normandy had always traded with each other and the duchy was by no means an important market. However, Orderic Vital, here probably following William of Poitiers for the last time, wrote of the period after 1070 :

The English and French lived peacefully together in the boroughs and towns and intermarried. You would see some places and markets full of French traders and goods, and everywhere you would notice that the English, who when they used to wear their native dress were considered uncouth by the French, were now affecting foreign fashions.

This is Poitiers' usual idealized picture. In any case outside the towns there was probably less civility. Some idea of the mould in which the new barons, King William's friends, were cast can be got from two contrasting character sketches, this time from Orderic's own pen. Of Hugh of Avranches, earl of Chester, he wrote:

This man, with the help of many cruel barons, shed much Welsh blood. He was not so much lavish as prodigal. His retinue was more like an army than a household, and in giving and receiving he kept no account. Each day he devastated his own land and preferred falconers and huntsmen to the cultivators of the soil and ministers of heaven. He was so much a slave to the gluttony of his belly that, weighed down by his fat, he could hardly move. From harlots he had many children of both sexes, who almost all came to an unfortunate end.

Later Orderic gives us another impression of Hugh's court:

He loved the world and all its pomps, which he regarded as the chief part of human happiness. For he was an active soldier, an extravagant giver, and took great pleasure in gaming and debauchery, and in jesters, horses and hounds, and other such vanities. An enormous household, which resounded with the noise of a crowd of youths, both noble and common, was always in attendance on him. Some good men, clerks as well as knights, also lived with him and rejoiced to share in his labours and wealth. In his chapel was Gerold, a clerk from Avranches, honest, religious, and well educated.

... This man tried hard to improve the conduct of the courtiers by setting before them the example of their ancestors. In many of them he saw, and censured, carnal lust, and he deplored the utter negligence that some showed in the worship of God. He uttered salutary warnings to the chief barons, the lesser knights, and the noble youths, and made a large collection from the Old Testament and more recent Christian histories of the campaigns of holy knights, to serve them as models. He recited excellently the struggles of Demetrius and of George, of Theodore and of Sebastian, of Duke Maurice and the Thebean legion, and of Eustace, the general-officer, and his men, all of whom by their martyrdom earned a crown in heaven. And he also told of the holy fighter William, who, after many campaigns, renounced the world, and under the monastic rule fought gloriously for the Lord.

Of Roger of Montgomery, earl of Shrewsbury, the patron of his own father, Odelerius of Orleans, who appears in the account, Orderic painted a glowing portrait:

He was wise and temperate and a lover of justice, and he loved the company of wise and sober men. He had with him for a long time three wise clerks, Godebald, Odelerius, and Herbert, to whose advice he profitably gave heed. To Warin the Bald, small in body but great in heart, he gave his niece, Armeira, in marriage and Shrewsbury castle, and Warin bravely defeated the Welsh and all other enemies and pacified the whole area entrusted to him. To other commands in the shire he appointed ... vassals who were all brave men. And helped by their understanding and strength Roger flourished greatly among the great magnates.

For a time the two nations stood apart, but they had the same religion and were not so different in culture that they could not come together. At first the future was unpredictable. The most likely eventuality was the absorption of the new masters and their way of life by the great and potent vernacular tradition. This had happened to the Normans themselves in France and would probably have come about quickly if England became separated again from Normandy and the Norman-English from their homelands. Like the king, the important new barons in England after 1066 were hardly settlers. Men like Eustace of Boulogne, Brian of Brittany, Robert of Mortain, Odo of Bayeux, William fitzOsbern, Hugh of Avranches, and Roger of Montgomery had no thought of cutting their ties with their places of origin. And although some of the adventurers, like Gherbod of Chester, threw up their acquisitions, the closeness of the homelands to England did not force them to make a choice of domicile and it was quite open to them to remain foreigners in England. But when they had more than one son there was the natural temptation to persuade the king to allow a geographical division. The heir could inherit the ancestral lands on the Continent and a younger son the 'conquest' in England. William fitzOsbern's estates were divided in this way after his death in 1071 and Roger of Montgomery's in 1094. The king made a similar arrangement in 1087. Had England been effectively separated from Normandy after William I's death, and the custom of dividing lands continued, then the Normans in England would probably have become English in a very short time. And besides the great men there were the many whose acquisitions in the kingdom were so much more important than their tiny fiefs in Normandy that almost from the beginning they must have been prepared to settle down.

Yet the anglicization of the newcomers was not inevitable. Conquering races can keep their culture relatively pure and can both exert pressure on, and set a pattern for imitation by, the subject peoples. The most striking peculiarity of the new aristocracy was that it spoke French. Probably some French had been spoken at Edward's court, even by Englishmen. William is said to have tried to learn to speak English; but after 1071 he had little incentive. Few English monoglots, except occasionally a bishop or abbot, were to be found in the court circle. The laity at court was almost exclusively French. Even in this context it is clear that had not the English nobles ruined themselves there would have been of necessity more rapid adjustments on both sides.

Besides French the newcomers brought with them a body of law and social custom which was their birth-right and which they had no thought of relinquishing. These Norman customs were at many points different from English, but often superficially. At the time the differences were important and it would be wrong to undervalue minor divergences. Sometimes a fairly rigid class system is externalized merely in subtle nuances of social behaviour. But when the differences are superficial, and at the mercy of fashion, changes occur which can have important social results. It was always possible, for example, that things English might become popular among the Normans, even that English women should appear especially desirable; and this attitude developed to some extent and in some directions among the second generation of the Norman-English. That none of the contrasts was too wide for compromise is shown by that supposed symbol of the new culture, the feudal knight. The horseman, or *chivaler*, was soon called in the kingdom a *cniht* (the retainer of the Old-English nobles), and the name endured. We may be sure from this that there was no fundamental difference between the *cniht* and the *chivaler* and that when men saw Count Robert of Mortain riding with his escort of *chivalers* he looked little different from their memory of Earl Harold riding with his *cnihtas*. The Normans were, perhaps, never so French as in England between 1066 and 1087; some of their customs were to take root in England and enrich the social pattern; some qualities, above all military virtues, they displayed exceptionally well; but there was nothing beyond their language to prevent them from merging into the traditional scene.

Owing to the accidents of later history the English aristocracy was to speak French for several centuries. But long before French was exerting its maximum influence in England language had ceased to be a racial distinction. French had simply become an aspect of polite society, and ability to speak it had spread down and was widely diffused. At the same time knowledge of English had seeped up. All those who were born and bred in the kingdom spoke some English and, except for the highest aristocracy, it quickly became the mother tongue. The English language was depressed—if at all—only for a short time. Most other cultural contributions of the Normans were accidental. The foreigners carried in, and were to remain carriers of, new fashions and movements which spread in France—fashions in architecture and in the art of war, religious and educational movements—most of which would have influenced the kingdom, although sometimes perhaps more slowly, conquest or no conquest. The Normans were both destroyers within an insular civilization of high value and conveyors of new ideas of the greatest potential. To draw up a balance sheet would be controversial and unprofitable.

Chapter Eight

Royal Government

FROM the beginning to the end of his career William
was a soldier. There is nothing to suggest that he had
intellectual interests or that he concerned himself with the
art or techniques of government and administration.
Government for him meant, beyond keeping the peace,
the enforcement of his rights, the loyalty of his subordinates, and the execution of his orders. Like his elder sons,
Robert Curthose and William Rufus, he was not an 'office
man'. He had no idea of privacy and little opportunity
for meditation. He could be interested, no doubt, in
practical problems of law, but even in this sphere he seems
to have preferred to use justiciars. If we compare him,
say, with his youngest son, Henry I, or his great-grandson,
Henry II, we appreciate how little was his zeal for statecraft and how rudimentary a ruler he was. To compare
him with future generations, with men educated in a
rapidly changing world, is, of course, unfair. But it makes
us realize that William was not ahead of his age, was, if
anything, a little archaic by the time of his death. One
virtue usually possessed by good soldiers is the ability to
give clear simple orders and to trust chosen subordinates
to carry them out successfully. There is every reason to
believe that William always knew what he wanted, had
loyal men available to do his will, and was able to drive
his projects through.

Not only did William bring a rather simple attitude to
government. He was also probably short of ideas. From
the little we can learn of Normandy and of William's rule
there it is reasonably clear that he was familiar with no
superior techniques to apply in the kingdom. Neither in
the ducal court nor in the localities were there skills, procedures, or officials which might serve as models in Eng-

land. Moreover, William had little time for the government of the kingdom. Once he had established order he was never there except when danger or disorder recalled him. In the intervals between fighting and hunting he had to make all sorts of decisions, but usually he must have acted on information provided by others. It is clear that William always had tremendous authority—he was more than the master, he was masterful—but equally clear that he normally operated at a level above the administrative. He gave the commands and it was for his servants to devise ways of carrying them out.

The first thing that William would have wanted to know after he had obtained the crown was what were his rights and powers. He had knowledgeable instructors. No one knew more of the secrets of Edward's government than Archbishops Stigand and Ealdred; and Earls Edwin, Morkere, and Waltheof were the sons and grandsons of earls. There were men at court who could testify to royal rights from the reign of Cnut, and also to the rights of bishops, abbots, earls, and thegns. Nor were there lacking men prepared to tell William what he should not do. Ealdred had administered the coronation oath and he was a brave man. It was remembered in his legend that he had not been afraid to withstand the king. It is inconceivable that William should not have taken over every right enjoyed by previous kings, and, as these were ample by contemporary standards, it is unlikely that he was dissatisfied with his inheritance or had conscious plans to extend the royal powers. Although the kingdom was in turmoil between 1066 and 1071 and the government was essentially military and arbitrary, William's need for English ecclesiastical support kept his rule within English traditions. When the purge of the episcopate took place in 1070, basic continuity had been achieved and, with the king soon an absentee, the pattern was unlikely to be drastically altered. But each king had his individuality, and it is the use made of royal rights which gives constitutional interest to any particular reign.

William certainly ruled differently from Edward. Because of a number of obvious factors he had after 1070 greater authority in the kingdom. 'He was a very stern and violent man, so that no one dared do anything against his will. . . . In his time people suffered much oppression and very many injuries.' And, breaking into verse, the English chronicler added, 'So fierce was the king that no hostility influenced him. All men had to follow his will entirely if they wished to live or keep their land.' We can accept that William was a hard ruler and sometimes, of necessity, acted arbitrarily. But when we scrutinize his actions, especially those of which men complained, we are often in doubt what precedent he was following and if he was really an innovator.

One clear innovation was the establishment of a royal forest. Edward, like his predecessors, had been a mighty hunter, but he seems to have been content to hunt over his own lands and only by invitation on the property of others. William must have had wider hunting rights than this as duke of Normandy, for in England he claimed to hunt where he chose and also to protect by law the beasts that he chased—the red and fallow deer and the roe, the wild boar, and perhaps the hare—together with the vert, the vegetation which harboured them. He physically extended his chase round Winchester, where he most often hunted, by depopulating part of Hampshire in order to create the New Forest. But, more important, he threw the royal monopoly and the forest law over large tracts of country irrespective of who held the land.

To be included in the royal forest, which was now the fate of many men and their farms, was an annoyance. The royal beasts, whatever damage they might do, could not be killed, and there were restrictions on the felling of timber, the clearing of thickets, and the keeping of dogs. Greater men, even if they had been accustomed to this monopoly in Normandy, found it irksome that they could hunt over their own lands only by royal licence. And we notice that each new king after the Conqueror had to agree at his accession to reduce the royal forest. But it was the church which was most critical of the forest law, partly, no doubt, because the clergy were subject to it and could not plead clerical immunity. What made it even worse was that hunting was forbidden to the clergy by canon law, and so no issue could be made of this odious royal policy. It is unlikely that William would have allowed a clerk to be mutilated for an offence against his forest; but the threat was there. And, besides, the church thought it indecent that the king should love the stags 'as if he were their father', and put a man's limbs in jeopardy for killing a wild animal. As a result William's destruction of a few settlements in Hampshire was regarded as even more heinous than his widespread military ravaging, and the church professed to see in the deaths of two of William's sons, Richard and Rufus, in the New Forest God's punishment for the act.

Just as William brought into England his own rights and customs, so each new settler carried his own law with him, a situation which could easily lead to a conflict of laws. One of the more authentic of William's enactments regulates the procedures to be followed in disputes between men of different race and deals especially with a mode of proof introduced by the Normans, the ordeal by combat. It was considered unfair that an Englishman should be forced to use a procedure to which he was unaccustomed, and it was enacted that, although when appropriate he could demand it from a Frenchman or employ it himself, he could not be compelled by a Frenchman to fight. Likewise, after the introduction of foreign prelates into the English church, William had to consider their position and special rights, and he ordered changes to be made in judicial procedure (which we consider in the next chapter). Invaders, however, are as liable to sudden death as to lawsuits, and William tried to protect his followers by imposing penalties on the murderer's lord, and then on the hundred in which the body was found, until the murderer was produced. In practice, except in the rare cases when the slayer was identified, this became a fine, *murdrum*, on the locality.

Other legal changes attributed to William are more doubtful. It was believed that he abolished the death penalty for all crimes and substituted mutilation. Although William is known to have had an aversion to killing except in war, it is hardly likely that he made such a sweeping change. He had Earl Waltheof beheaded in 1076 and certainly by Henry I's reign thieves and robbers were being hanged in large numbers. The supposed enactment is more likely to be a later view of William's ordinary practice. William differed from his English predecessors in his treatment of political offenders, possibly because he was more troubled than they by rebellion and more concerned with prisoners of war. Judicial executions of nobles had been very rare in England—the execution of Eadric Streona in 1017 is one of the few recorded—and no example can be cited of imprisonment. Edward the Confessor outlawed or exiled all who incurred his wrath. English kings had no castles and so no prisons. William, on the other hand, both as duke and king, had castles, and they were often bulging with prisoners. Since imprisonment was costly he normally had lesser political offenders mutilated. The treatment of the rebels in England in 1075 is a good example of William's practice.

Finally it was believed that William forbade the selling of slaves outside the kingdom. According to William of Malmesbury either Bishop Wulfstan or Archbishop Lanfranc forced this measure on an unwilling king. But again it is doubtful whether in fact this law was enacted by William, especially as Wulfstan is found leading a moral crusade at Bristol against the Irish slave trade and fighting it with preaching and not by legal process.

It will be seen that William's deliberate alterations of English law were few in number and, except for the introduction of forest law, almost entirely confined to procedure. He did not innovate unnecessarily. For example, although he was a strong supporter in Normandy of the Truce of God, an ecclesiastical measure to control warfare, he saw no reason to introduce it into the kingdom. Like Edward, and unlike Cnut, William was no legislator. He granted to the English their own laws and he accepted with the kingdom the shire and hundred courts in which English law ran. Similarly he took it for granted that the French would enjoy their own customs. But as Norman law was little different from English, the two could lie side by side until they amalgamated or were both superseded by new processes, just as English and Scandinavian law, together with other provincial customs, had existed, and to some extent were still existing, in peaceful conjunction. Each man his own law was a basic assumption of the period.

As William accepted the rights of Edward the Confessor and added little to them, it remains to be considered whether by his behaviour or unexpressed attitude he changed the conception of English kingship, whether he created a new monarchy. It is sometimes held that William introduced a new feature into English monarchy, feudal lordship, and that after the Conquest two different types of relationship were brought together : a king with his subjects and a lord with his vassals—rather like the effigies on William's seal where he appears, on the reverse, enthroned in majesty as king of England, and, on the obverse, galloping on horseback as duke of Normandy. In its more extreme forms this view is clearly false, for Edward likewise had been the lord of men, and one of the thickest strands in Germanic kingship was the personal relationship between the lord king and his companions and followers. But we may assume that English kingship, as interpreted by a Norman duke, would show some change, and it is possible to see in the sum of the individual relationships between the king and his barons, and they with theirs, each guaranteed by homage and fealty, a new contractual society of the greatest constitutional significance. Each man had duties and rights towards another; each vassal could renounce his fealty and lawfully resist if his rights were disregarded; each lord could despoil his man if the duties were not performed. Hence from the Norman Conquest there was a direct line to Henry I's coronation charter and so to Magna Carta. A new dynamic, based on stress and counter-stress, had appeared in the kingdom which was to produce a constitution.

The view has its place in constitutional history. It is, however, an abstraction which hardly serves to explain the observable events. Neither William himself, nor his successors, allowed this right of opposition to his barons. If they rebelled, however just the cause, they were simply guilty of rebellion, and he broke them. Nor can it be claimed that homage and fealty introduced a stronger loyalty than had the Old-English ceremonies of subordination. Barons rebelled against William and his sons rather more frequently than had been the case before 1066. Moreover William subscribed to no 'feudal theory'. In 1086 at Salisbury he took oaths of fealty from all important landowners irrespective of their tenure. This had probably been English practice and it could also have been Norman. But it makes a mockery of a constitutional theory based on an ideal view of feudalism. All that we can confidently say is that each generation of the new baronage considered that the king was too harsh, insisted too much on his own rights, and paid insufficient attention to their own, and that whenever the monarchy was weak, especially when a new king succeeded, demanded the abolition of bad customs and a recognition of their own liberties. These protests are of constitutional importance. But it may be that they were the answer to typically strong English royal government rather than based on a new contractual theory.

On the whole it seems that William's monarchy was Edward's run at full power. There were changes in detail and in tone; but to emphasize these at the expense of the basic continuity of the office is to falsify the picture.

Two directions in which William certainly increased the pressure were taxation and military service. England was unique in Western Europe in that the king could collect a tax from almost all land. As a result of provincial, shire-, and hundredal assessments, most estates were assessed for royal taxation in terms of hides, carucates, or sulungs, and the tax was collected at so many pence or shillings on these units. Geld was in appearance similar to the modern 'rates'—a property tax paid on an assessed rateable value. Traditionally geld was imposed to maintain the king's mercenary army and fleet against Viking marauders, and Edward had ceased to collect it after 1051 when he had disbanded his hired navy. William, who was using large mercenary forces, reimposed the tax at a high rate and apparently every year. No wonder the English chronicler lamented that the king 'deprived his underlings of many a mark of gold and more hundreds of pounds of silver, which he took by weight and with great injustice from his people, with little justification for such a deed. He fell into avarice and loved greediness above all.'

Military service, too, seems usually to have been based on the hidage, and certainly in some areas estates had to provide one soldier for each five hides. Again this custom may have fallen into partial disuse owing to the peacefulness of Edward's reign, only to be revived and exploited by William. English armies were in the field under Norman commanders from 1068 and fought as far away as Maine and the Vexin. Orderic Vital several times claims that William found 60,000 soldiers in England, especially as a result of the Domesday Inquest. At any rate he found soldiers and had them drilled and used by his barons. Otherwise these could never have brought adequate contingents to the royal army.

Although it is now the fashion to regard Domesday Book as purely descriptive—a child of the king's curiosity about the kingdom he had won—there is much to be said for the old-fashioned view that the main purpose of the Domesday Inquest of 1086 was to discover and record the hidage, the rateable value, of all estates and so disclose the liability to geld and military service. The survey served many subsidiary purposes, but William's commissioners concerned themselves basically with two matters. First the liability to geld and the existing rateable value of each estate (How many hides?), and secondly its past, current, and potential commercial value. It is this latter aspect which gives the survey so much bulk and interest, for in connexion with commercial value much statistical information (the area under cultivation, manpower, stock and equipment, and exploitable resources) was collected and in part retained for record. That these two matters, rateable and true value, were investigated must imply that William's purpose went beyond conservation of his rights and that he was looking to see if he could either increase or rationalize the assessments or increase the demands made upon them. The survey was designed to discover past evasion, to prevent it in the future, and to provide the economic data on which a revision of the assessments could be based.

The survey furnished other information useful to the king. Often royal rights in the shires and boroughs were listed. For the first time William had a complete picture of the area and value of his own estates and of those of his tenants-in-chief: he had a cadastral survey which could be used whenever he wished to make new enfeoffments. He had also an analysis of the tenurial relationships in the kingdom—he learned who held what of whom. As the investigation progressed a large number of disputed claims to land came to light which had to be settled by litigation. Thus Domesday Book is also a register of titles to land.

The Domesday survey is the greatest administrative achievement of William's government. Nothing like it had been seen in any barbarian country and it was long before such an effort could be attempted elsewhere or repeated in England. The impulse was undoubtedly William's; it was carried out by the king's administrative officers; and its execution was possible because of national danger. The machinery used for the survey is often regarded as the introduction from France of *missi dominici*, royal itinerant investigators, using the equally foreign juries of recognition, bodies of neighbours sworn to answer questions truthfully from their own knowledge. Recent studies, however, chiefly Professor Galbraith's, have shown how complex the machinery was, and have emphasized the 'paper work' more than the public verification of the statistics. It seems best to regard the survey as a unique administrative achievement contrived out of the collective wisdom of William's advisers. The words of the English chronicler are well known. At Christmas 1085, when William held his court at Gloucester, 'the king had much thought and very deep discussion with his council about this country—how it was occupied or with what sort of people. Then he sent his men all over England into every shire and had them find out how many hundred hides there were in the shire . . .' Such a survey had never been attempted before in England or Normandy, and we must believe that Archbishop Lanfranc and the bishops and barons, when ordered to carry it out, drew on every possible experience and memory in order to improvise an administrative method. Basically they collected the information in writing from the tenants-in-chief, who themselves called on their own councils and officials—the stewards, reeves, and 'farmers'—and then checked the facts, especially doubtful or disputed matters, both by correspondence and by empanelling local juries. Every administrative official in the kingdom, royal and baronial, was involved in the collection of the information; and the statistics were first digested at regional centres (the Exeter Domesday is an example of one of these reports) and then, except for the East-Anglian survey, further compressed at Winchester into the final record.

We cannot believe that the ducal government could have carried out such a project. It was the work of the English royal administration, using English administrative units, and possibly English techniques. The directive ideas, however, could have come from anywhere—from prelates who employed the written record and because of their book learning had a greater memory and better acquaintance with other countries, or from lay barons who had common sense and knew what could be done in the shires. Norman Sicily, with its remnants of imperial government and Arabic skills, may have furnished some ideas. But the exact precedents for each procedure have not yet been established and may always remain in doubt. Nor is the inquest's importance as a precedent clear, since it was not until the late twelfth century that surveys, and on a much smaller scale, were started again. We should probably content ourselves with using the Domesday survey as a proof of some conspicuous merits possessed by William's government in England : the king's incisiveness and large vision and the competence and ingenuity of the administration. The survey itself was probably completed between January and August 1086 and some of the information was presented to William before he made his final departure from the kingdom. Whether this wonderful description was really useful to the government, or much used, is another matter. The fine condition of the manuscript shows that it has been handled more by scholars than by clerks.

Because of the nature of William's rule the subordinate level of government is of special interest. During the king's absences from Normandy there seems usually to have been in the duchy an informal regency council of some trusted barons under the nominal head of Queen Matilda or

Robert Curthose, the king's heir. In England the pattern was modified. In 1067 William appointed two military commanders, William fitzOsbern and Odo of Bayeux. But after 1071 there was usually a small baronial council under a bishop. Normally Lanfranc, archbishop of Canterbury, was recognized, or appointed, president. When he was not available Odo of Bayeux, Walkelin of Winchester, or some other prelate was given responsibility. Geoffrey of Coutances was another who did much work for William. There were probably several reasons for this policy. William had no wish to create appanages for his sons, and although after 1077 he may well have decided to bequeath England to William Rufus, his second son, he liked to have his faithful company. Similarly William needed the military service in Normandy of the leading English barons, and he often took them with him. But, above all, in the kingdom he put greater trust in prelates than in barons. He had immediately given great regional responsibilities to Æthelwig, abbot of Evesham, and Ealdred, archbishop of York. In 1076 he appointed Walcher, bishop of Durham, earl of Northumbria. And whenever there was a crisis in England he looked to the bishops. He had made Lanfranc 'primate of All Britain' and always intervened to enforce the subjection of the archbishop of York to Canterbury. The natural inference is that William wished Lanfranc to have a clear titular superiority to support his vice-regal position. Also, Lanfranc was usually resident in the kingdom and his occasional visit to Rome was only grudgingly allowed. Moreover, with Odo, the king's brother, nearly always in command of an army in England, and Lanfranc, the king's servant, in political control, and neither much loving the other, the kingdom could not be safer against plot and insurrection. This is one reason why William was so bitter when Odo betrayed his trust in 1082.

Subject to William's general directives and arbitrary interferences the overall government of England was in ecclesiastical hands from 1072 until 1087. The effect of this influential position on the English church itself will be investigated later. Its effect on secular government can be considered neutral. Prelates had the intellectual ability to innovate but also were sensitive to tradition and almost always amenable to the king. It is difficult to point to any of William's secular measures in England for which the church was responsible and easy to instance some which cannot have pleased churchmen. In general it would seem that episcopal ministers in England served the general trend of William's policy which was to enjoy all his rights in a peaceful kingdom.

William brought at least a nucleus of household servants with him to England, but the few who would accompany him on campaign and even those who could rejoin him after the first expedition were hardly adequate to help him rule the kingdom. William improvised between 1067 and 1071. Just as he assumed Edward's rights so he accepted those of Harold's servants who suited him. But the Norman and then the Angevin kings, however many provinces they ruled, had only one household. Separate local administrations might be created for the several units, but the king did not radically change his personal servants as he travelled from area to area. Hence Edward's and Harold's body and domestic servants quickly disappeared. William would not want Englishmen round his person, and Norman stewards, butlers, chamberlains, constables, and marshals remained in service or were recruited as necessary. At the same time some of the local staff in the various halls and palaces were retained. William's treatment of Edward's clerical servants was, of necessity, different. The duke had his own priests and clerks, but he had no seal, no writing office, and no records. Archbishop Stigand probably offered the services of Edward's clerks almost complete, and, as William's original aim was to take over the government as a going concern, the offer was accepted. It was not long before William was rewarding one of Edward's most important clerks, Regenbald of Cirencester, with land. There had been a tradition of long service among clerks in the Old-English royal household. The clerks knew the secrets of royal government, the king's rights and how they were administered and enforced. They could draft and seal writs, notifications of grants of land and rights; they could probably turn their hand to drawing up a land-book, a more solemn title to land guaranteed by the church and the *witan*; and they knew all about chirographs, the appropriate documentation for private contracts, especially for the lease of land. They also understood geld and military service, English law, and English jurisdictional procedure. During the transitional period these English clerks (not all English by birth) were essential to the new king.

After 1071, when William was usually in Normandy, English clerks lost some of their value. William's other clerks had learned the techniques and fewer Englishmen were required in William's ambulatory court. Some were dispensed with; some, perhaps, were attached to the regency council. At all events there remained a single household and a single itinerant secretariat. By this time some changes are apparent. Accustomed to Frankish royal practice William regarded his clerical servants as serving his ducal or royal chapel with the title of chaplains, and quite early as king introduced (from France, not from Normandy) the office of chancellor, the writing master who was a member of the chapel. The chancellor, or his deputy, not only had the custody of the king's seal, but also was in charge of the chaplains, and so William appointed his own trusted men to this office : Herfast (promoted to be bishop of Elmham in 1070), Osmund (bishop of Salisbury 1078), Maurice archdeacon of Le Mans (bishop of London 1085), and finally Gerard precentor of Rouen (promoted to Hereford by Rufus and to York by Henry I). The reorganization was important for it determined future development. But in the beginning there was little more than a change in nomenclature. William took over at first the English secretariat because it was far more advanced than his own, and simply gave it a Frankish appearance. There were hardly any secretarial novelties in William's reign, and nothing that would suggest that the new men had new or superior ideas. The traditional writs were issued (although very occasionally in Latin instead of in English), and in the dioceses the old-fashioned 'landbook' continued to be drawn up. William's seal and coinage were modelled on the English. By the time that William could shed some of his English cares the old traditions had been confirmed with little modification and

William's deputies in England were in no position to disturb them.

Around the king and his household was his council, a fluctuating body of men who kept him company, gave him advice, and helped him with lawsuits. Men came in and went out of court according to circumstances. Where the king was there was his court and council. There is nothing to suggest that William's courts differed greatly from Edward's except in personnel. Until 1071 there were English nobles at court; but William always gave most trust to his bishops and a few intimate barons. It may be that under Lanfranc's influence there was sometimes a clearer division between secular and ecclesiastical business. For example, after the Christmas court 1085, when the Domesday survey was decided, the prelates held a more private meeting for three days. But this was probably only a matter of convenience—they had business to discuss which would not have interested the barons—rather than the expression of a principle.

William of Malmesbury, translating Coleman, gives us a description of a royal court on the River Parret in Somerset probably at North or South Petherton, both royal manors, and probably in 1070 or 1071, to hear a case brought by Wulfstan, the old bishop of Worcester, against Thomas, the new Norman archbishop of York. Wulfstan claimed the return of twelve villages which Thomas' predecessor, Archbishop Ealdred, had retained after his promotion from Worcester to York; and we are told that in this large assembly of magnates Bishop Odo of Bayeux and all the barons supported Thomas, and only Lanfranc favoured Wulfstan. The parties took their stand and the case was opened. Wulfstan, the plaintiff, presumably stated his case, and then Thomas withdrew with his advisers to compose his reply. Wulfstan slept during the adjournment and, although woken by his councillors when Thomas returned to plead both acutely and copiously, instead of paying attention merely recited psalms. He was then in his turn ordered out so that he could, with the advice of his council, prepare his answer to Thomas' defence (technically Wulfstan's replication), but on leaving the court recited the office of nones and, when urged by his men that there were more urgent matters on hand, confided the justice of his cause to God and to the saints who had been bishops of Worcester. Accordingly when he returned to court and the king asked what counsel he had obtained, he answered, 'My counsel rests with you.' Whereupon William, through the influence of Lanfranc, gave judgment for the plaintiff. Wulfstan's solitariness and confidence are clearly heightened in order to prove the serenity of the saint; but that the sympathy of the court was with the Norman we need not doubt. All the same William gave Wulfstan the verdict. He was the judge and no votes were counted.

It was William's custom to observe the three greatest ecclesiastical feasts—Easter, Whitsun, and Christmas—with a special court and usually in a monastery because of the religious ceremonies. This was common Frankish practice and had been observed by English kings and Norman dukes alike. The king sat enthroned in majesty, wearing his crown and bearing all the regalia; the archbishop celebrated a votive mass; and the *laudes*, the hymn of adulation to the king—*Willelmo serenissimo, a Deo consecrato, magno et pacifico regi, vita et victoria!*—was chanted. These great courts served several purposes. There was the adoration of the anointed king, God's vicar on earth, the feasting of the assembled magnates (archbishops and bishops, abbots and earls, thegns and knights, according to the English chronicler writing under 1087), and also the transaction of important business. The Old-English chronicler tells us that as often as the king was in England he held the Easter feast at Winchester, Whitsun at Westminster, and Christmas at Gloucester (all monasteries). Certainly William aimed at visiting Winchester at Easter, presumably for the English revenue accounts rendered at the principal royal treasury, and in his last months in England, Christmas 1085 to Whitsun 1086, he kept to the ideal itinerary; but his visits to Westminster and Gloucester were far from regular.

When William was out of England there was no royal court and probably no royal seal in the kingdom. But as most government was local there was no interregnum : a large number of overlapping and often interchangeable

authorities simply carried on. There was the regency council, which could receive orders from the king and transmit
them to the appropriate local officials, and, in an emergency, act on its own initiative. There were the bishops
who could be expected to take orders from Lanfranc. On
the frontiers were the earls. And in the shires were the
sheriffs, the custodians of the royal castles, and sometimes
local justiciars. Besides these royal officials there were the
barons, each ruling his own honour and possessing some
fragments of royal authority, hundredal jurisdiction and
other legal rights which were recognized as enjoyed by
delegation or concession from the king. Except for the
castellans and probably the local justiciars, the situation
was largely as it had been under Edward. Nor does it seem
that William made far-reaching changes. He appointed
his own men to the various offices, improvised from time
to time, and from his experience and caution probably
unconsciously contrived a fragmentation of authority and
a balance of powers.

The collection of the royal revenue from the demesne,
the boroughs, and the king's many debtors and tributaries
remained a duty of the sheriffs and their servants; and the
royal treasuries continued to use the traditional methods
of account. The Domesday Survey may be regarded as
implying some criticism of the financial administration
and even perhaps as preparing for a major reform. But
William was dead before he could act. An earlier and
more pressing problem was the provision of adequate
justice in the kingdom. The shire courts were dislocated
as a result of the conquest. Many of the suitors who knew
the law had been dispossessed and replaced by foreigners.
And the tenurial upheaval had increased the volume of
litigation. The general disorganization which followed the
coming of the Normans, the disputes over boundaries,
tenures, and rights, could easily lead to high-handed
action unless the courts could offer speedy justice. There
was also an increase in crime. All contemporary writers
emphasize William's zeal for order and justice. He was
fully alive to the problem of providing courts and judges,
and he showed the utmost ingenuity in judicial administration. His aim was not to reform the old judicial system,

the shire and hundred courts, but to keep it working under exceptional conditions. There was a period of improvisation, and the Conqueror's special arrangements did not furnish many precedents for his successors.

If we glance at the position as a whole we shall notice a wide dispersal of authority, so characteristic of the period, and the presence of a number of unspecialized officials. The new sheriffs were sometimes justiciars and often castellans as well. Appointed by the king mostly from the baronage of the second rank, they were great men in their shires. But William often changed them—Domesday Book frequently notices a succession of sheriffs—and there were men who kept a close watch over them. Urse d'Abitot, sheriff of Worcestershire, was cursed by Archbishop Ealdred and sometimes provoked Bishop Wulfstan. There were also the barons of the shire who resented too much shrieval power. Roger, earl of Hereford, rebelled when William sent royal sheriffs to hear pleas in his earldom. Many of William's writs concerning tenure of lands, services, and liberties were, we notice, addressed jointly to the sheriff and an important baron in the shire. The castellans do not seem to have been used for administrative purposes, but they were, with the sheriff, a check on the military power of the barons. This balance between different authorities is typical of the Old-English kingdom and that it continued in a slightly different form under William was no accident. It made the king the supreme arbiter.

Which of William's virtues and achievements are stressed or praised depends much on the attitude of the beholder. If the Old-English kingdom is considered in decay then William's changes are emphasized. If, on the contrary, William is considered the barbarian who conquered a civilized kingdom the tendency is to minimize his adaptations and give him scant praise for his conservatism. The safest course is to enquire how far William achieved his ends. If we accept that he had no real desire to transform the government of England, that he had no superior techniques to introduce, and that his agents, although talented, were not administrative geniuses, we shall probably grant that his true success was to have kept the government going, collected the royal revenue, dispensed adequate justice, and secured tolerable good order despite the shattering disturbances of 1066-71. Notwithstanding occasional mistakes and sporadic shows of impatience, even of exasperation, William's basic aim was to acquire, not to disturb. Inevitably in the circumstances in which he won the kingdom many novelties were introduced. In the beginning there seemed to be a mounting storm of change which might easily lead to a complete reconstruction. Yet, when the tempest had subsided and much of the wreckage had been repaired, vast tracts of the old scene were still recognizable and the damaged areas had been rebuilt in a way which, although foreign, was not completely strange. William improvised at every stage in order to keep the kingdom intact and profitable. Some of his measures were drawn from his experience as duke in a Frankish kingdom or from the background of his foreign advisers, some seem to have been no more than adroit reactions to individual problems. William showed his skill in preventing the collapse of his conquest. Soldiering shaded into government and government was soldiering tamed. Medieval society had enormous powers of recuperation largely because of the simplicity of the economy and the crudity of the organization. Military government was typical and usually necessary.

Chapter Nine

William and the English Church

WILLIAM acquired with England an ancient church, rich in traditions, and respected and influential in the kingdom. It was also superficially quite unlike the Norman church. Its buildings were archaic in style, small and cramped, yet contained remarkable treasures; its ministers were mostly exponents of a vernacular culture; and its saints had uncouth names. There were also those many small differences in custom and ritual which can arouse so much passion. Moreover there had been recent laxity in observing the various Rules, some irregularity, and a misunderstanding with the church of Rome. Although in 1066 the English church was not flourishing, it was orthodox, respectable, and artistic, it was, if not on the eve of reform, at least easily reformable, and it contained some outstanding prelates : Stigand of Canterbury, an archbishop without a pallium, reaching the end of a somewhat enigmatic career, but talented and influential with the kings since Cnut; Ealdred of York, another worldly bishop, and one whose skill in statecraft and military affairs made him immediately familiar and welcome to the Normans; Wulfstan of Worcester, the perfect representative of the insular civilization, whose simplicity and loyalty earned the Conqueror's trust, and canonization in the twelfth century.

This church lay at William's mercy. The English clergy were trained in loyalty, and, except for a very few exceptions, were prepared to accept the conqueror without cavil. The bishops convincingly proved their loyalty to their new master in the years of disorder—only the bishop of Durham became involved in the rebellions—and the abbots, although more provoked and less reliable, did not defect as a whole. The leading bishops may well have expected at least tolerance from the victor as a reward for their services; but this was a vain hope. To some extent William flattered only to deceive. A number of reasons made his intervention, at a suitable opportunity, inevitable. He regarded the ducal, and so the royal, church as pertaining to his demesne and was accustomed to regulating its affairs. Since he intended to rely much on bishops for his government it was essential that they should be men whom he understood. Abbots he required to be much less worldly than bishops, to be the salt of the church, and English abbots he soon realized had lost their savour. He was committed to reform and the monasteries would have to be shaken up. William also was the kind of conventional Christian who was displeased by unfamiliar customs; and, besides, he was temperamentally averse to the types of indulgence prevalent in the English church. Finally there was the pressure from all those who wanted a share in the ecclesiastical spoils, ducal clerks clamouring for the higher English benefices and reforming monks who coveted the chance to set the monasteries right. If Stigand believed that he could withstand all this weight, and it seems that he did, his memory of past successes had dimmed his judgment.

Until 1070 William relied heavily on the native church and its leaders, and only offended by confiscating such treasure as he required to reward those churches which had aided his expedition and to subsidise his own military expenses. He put great trust in Ealdred of York and in at least one abbot, Æthelwig of Evesham, and he treated Stigand with elaborate respect. He even allowed Stigand in 1067 to consecrate a bishop to the vacant see of Dorchester, and that William chose a monk of Fécamp would have caused Stigand no surprise or alarm. In 1070 William broke the agreement. The various pressures on him to take action were mounting and the moment was propitious. Ealdred of York had died, the rebellions had lost momentum, many Normans had been enfeoffed with English estates, and a purge of the highest level in the English church would neither weaken the Conqueror's position nor lead to increased unrest.

It was decided to start with the deposition of some

native bishops. With new direction at the top a reform could follow. So, as in the case of Archbishop Mauger in 1054–5, William invited the pope to send legates to give effect to his royal plans. Alexander II, although ill-informed and prejudiced by the information laid, at least sent an experienced servant, Ermenfrid, bishop of Sitten, supported by two cardinal-priests. The bishop had some acquaintance with Norman and English affairs, for he had operated against Mauger and in 1062 had probably been sent to England with Archbishop Ealdred to inspect the church and enforce some agreed reforms. On arrival in 1070 the legates sent summonses to all the bishops to attend with the abbots of their diocese a council at Winchester on 7 April, 'so that we may cut down those things that wax evilly in the vineyard of the Lord of Sabaoth and plant those that will be beneficial to the health of both souls and bodies.' The bishops and abbots must have assembled in fear.

The legates seem to have come with instructions to depose Archbishop Stigand and all bishops consecrated by him. These did not meet William's requirements, for the first of his new men had been consecrated by Stigand and there were bishops with impeccable orders who had been marked down. William got his way. Afterwards Alexander II was not entirely satisfied that justice had been done, or at least that all proper formalities had been observed. But his worried letters had no effect. Possibly because political motives rather than canonical reasons prevailed, the exact charges brought against those condemned have not been transmitted. Stigand himself seems to have been charged with intrusion, obtaining a pallium from a false pope, and pluralism. In the case of the bishops who were deposed we can only suggest the political reasons: Æthelmaer of East Anglia because he was Stigand's brother, Æthelwine of Durham because he had joined the Northumbrian rebels, and Æthelric of Selsey because of the strategic importance of his diocese. Leofwine of Lichfield, a married monk, resigned in order to avoid deposition. Of the twelve of Edward's bishops still surviving in 1070 seven were spared, of whom only two or three were native born.

To fill the vacant sees William made five appointments

in 1070, one in the following year, and two in 1072 (one consequent on the death of the bishop of Exeter). In the rest of the reign there were nine further vacancies. Rochester, which lost two bishops by death, was under the patronage of the archbishop of Canterbury, and each time Lanfranc nominated a monk from his old house, Bec. In all William made sixteen appointments to twelve sees. As he promoted no Englishman we may assume that this was his policy, and as he chose thirteen clerks out of his own chapel and only three monks we can believe that in general he held that bishoprics should normally be a reward for personal service to the king and that monks were unfitted to rule a diocese. In William's reign usually a third of the fifteen bishops were monks; but the proportion became even more unfavourable under his sons. The men promoted were mostly Normans, but two Lotharingian clerks, Walcher to Durham in 1071 and Robert Losinga to Hereford in 1079, and one monk from Maine (but probably of Norman origin), William of St Calais to Durham in 1080, also received William's favour. William's policy of denationalizing the English episcopate was achieved quickly because those of Edward's bishops who were spared were mostly foreign. In 1072 there were eight Normans, four Lotharingians, two Englishmen, and one Italian on the bench. By 1078 the Normans had increased to ten and by 1087 to eleven, the Lotharingians being reduced to three and then two, and the English to one. The elimination of Edward's men, was, however, slower. Of the fifteen bishops in 1072 six had served Edward in that rank and a further two as clerks. By 1080 half these remained and in 1087 there were still three. William had achieved his aim without destroying all continuity.

As William appointed almost exclusively clerks out of his household it is clear that the new bishops were his personal choice. No trace of Archbishop Lanfranc's influence can be seen, except in the case of Rochester, and all that we can allow him is a possible right of veto. William not only chose his bishops but also enfeoffed them with their office by handing them their episcopal ring and staff. Edward's practice is not known with certainty. His attitude was similar to William's, but it is possible that the use of this particular form of investiture was a Norman innovation. Reformers were already denouncing it as an objectionable symbol of secular domination over the church, and William's son, Henry I, was forced to discontinue the ceremony. In choosing—'electing'—his bishops William was only following Norman and English custom, indeed, current practice. Likewise in investing the bishops-elect and taking homage and fealty from them, so that they became his vassals, he was exercising ancestral rights and hardly diverging in spirit from English custom. He was, however, free from some common secular vices. He did not prolong vacancies in order to enjoy the revenues of the sees. The number of bishops dropped to twelve in 1085, but the situation was quickly righted. His record in this respect is exemplary. More important, he did not sell bishoprics, and it was the heresy of simony, rather than other irregularities, which was the main target of the 'Hildebrandine' reformers at this time. They were prepared to tolerate much secular interference, even domination, provided that the ruler's hands were clean and his control was benevolent. We do not know how aware William was of the critical attitude to the old order developing in some continental ecclesiastical circles. But we can be sure that he would have been deaf to their views. He knew his rights and did not intend to abandon any of them.

From William's appointments to the episcopal bench in England we can see what qualities he looked for : at least respectable conduct, sympathy towards ecclesiastical reform, administrative and, if possible, military skill, and loyalty to the new order, especially to the king. Bishoprics were certainly not to be the spoil of the Norman baronial families; they were to be the reward for ducal and royal servants. William's promotions in 1070–2 are of great interest because presumably he was then on his best behaviour. All the bishops-elect were royal clerks and we notice a considerable range in ecclesiastical merit. Walkelin, appointed to Winchester, was a good bishop by any standard; the immorality and waywardness of Herfast, William's chancellor, promoted to Elmham, were scandalous. The other four bishops fall within this range. These appointments were not such as to earn William any real reputation as an ecclesiastical reformer. We may assume that he demanded higher qualities from his archbishops. Since the deposition of Mauger he had taken the greatest care over Rouen. It was the custom in England, and a course which had been adopted by William in 1067, to promote to the archsees a diocesan bishop who had proved himself worthy. As William broke with this tradition in 1070 we may think that, for one reason or another, he considered none of the Norman bishops suitable. The choice of his clerk, Thomas, canon of Bayeux, a protégé of Bishop Odo, for the archbishopric of York cannot be faulted. Thomas, a scholar and musician, enjoyed a reputation similar to Walkelin's.

It is Lanfranc's appointment to Canterbury that calls for most explanation. This monk was at least approaching his sixtieth year, had accepted all promotion with reluctance, is believed to have refused Rouen in 1067, and was without diocesan experience. On his record he was hardly the man for the task. There is much to suggest that William's half-brother, Odo, bishop of Bayeux and already earl of Kent, expected this natural culmination of his career. A generation earlier it would have been the obvious step. In 1070 it was impossible for several reasons: William cannot have wanted another Mauger of Rouen; Pope Alexander II would have vetoed the translation because of Odo's unsuitability for high ecclesiastical office. The pope may, indeed, have suggested Lanfranc. In any case, it is likely that Lanfranc's unworldliness and pliability were just the qualities that William was looking for—the king would rule the church—and that William regarded Lanfranc's great reputation as a theologian and teacher the perfect cover for the deficiencies of some of his new bishops. The pope admired Lanfranc as *magister artium*; the Norman monasteries were bound to applaud the royal wisdom; and Lanfranc, through his controversy with Berengar, was a symbol of orthodoxy. William could not have proclaimed more obviously his moral intentions in England. Lanfranc showed the expected reluctance to undertake the great burden, at first was often bewildered, dismayed, and indecisive, but he outlived his master and grew slowly into his high office. He became the best arch-bishop of Canterbury since Dunstan, whom in some ways he resembled.

William had at least the good sense to put the best men into the most important sees, and this was an attitude of which all contemporaries approved. If we look at William's English appointments as a whole we may allow that three of the sixteen gained more than a contemporary reputation : Lanfranc; Osmund, bishop of Salisbury in 1078, William's chancellor, the liturgist who was later canonized; and the Lotharingian Robert Losinga, bishop of Hereford in 1079, an important scholar and a close friend of St Wulfstan of Worcester. Lanfranc's nominee to Rochester in 1077, Gundulf, monk and architect, should be added to these. On the other hand, only one of William's appointments was disgraceful, and few of his bishops enjoyed no reputation at all.

William's record may be considered better than Edward's, if only because of his imaginativeness in select-ing Lanfranc for Canterbury. But it is hardly in a com-pletely different class. Ealdred will stand comparison with Thomas, Herman of Sherborne with Walkelin or Osmund. And William appointed no one who can be compared with Wulfstan of Worcester. By promoting largely from the royal chapel William limited his choice. The newcomers, because they came in as new brooms and often took over a diocese and see ravaged by war, dis-turbed by the changes in the nobility, and neglected owing to the aftermath of the conquest, had to reorganize and reform. And because they were little affected by the English past they could change ruthlessly. Some were dis-satisfied with the site of their cathedral church, and looked for a more important town into which to move their see. Almost all, in emulation of each other, prepared to de-molish their cathedral churches and rebuild in a more familiar style. Even Wulfstan, in tears, was persuaded to destroy the church of St Mary which his great and admired predecessor, St Oswald, had built. Similarly with the cathedral chapters. The first movement of those new-comers who were clerks and who received a monastic see was either to break the connexion with the cathedral priory or even to suppress the convent. Walkelin threatened the old minster at Winchester with suppression and was only prevented by the stubbornness of the monks, supported by Lanfranc and the pope. The Normans also disliked the semi-monastic organization of some of the reformed secular minsters, where a common fund and communal sleeping and dining arrangements had been the rule; and these customs they were able to break, substituting individual houses and prebends for the canons and gradually the 'four-square' constitution of dignitaries —dean, treasurer, precentor, and chancellor (master of the schools).

These changes, whether or not they were improvements, reveal bustling men who knew what they liked and at first tried their utmost to recreate the accustomed scene so that they should feel at home. Occasionally the conditions were intractable, sometimes the first intolerance was gradually worn down. It would be a mistake to think that the episcopal bench was split on racial grounds. Coleman has a story of Wulfstan and Geoffrey of Coutances which has the full flavour of this mixed society. Wulfstan was always modestly dressed, and on one occasion, possibly at court, Geoffrey made good natured fun of the saint, and asked him why, when he could and should wear sable, beaver, or wolf, he went clad in lamb-skins. Wulfstan replied that while it was proper that Geoffrey and others replete with secular wisdom should use the skins of cunning animals, he, who was without subterfuge, was content with his lamb-skins. And when Geoffrey still joked and suggested that he should at least wear cat-skins, Wulfstan said, 'Believe me, we chant more often of the lamb of God than of His cat.' This answer amused Geoffrey enormously. The two bishops, we notice, although poles apart in culture and character, respected one another and could indulge in semi-affectionate badinage in which there was nevertheless some criticism of the other's behaviour. This was the tolerance of men who had got to know each other. With Robert, bishop of Hereford, Wulfstan became on terms of spiritual intimacy, and it was Robert, warned by a vision while at court, who hastened back to conduct Wulfstan's funeral service. On the other hand it is clear from the book of miracles, that many Normans, because of Wulfstan's birth, required special proof of his holiness.

It was English custom that the king with the advice of his *witan*, clerical and lay, should promulgate ecclesiastical legislation. But after the astonishing output of the years 942–1023 there was a lull, for the law had been declared. There may, however, have been some episcopal injunctions, for Archbishop Ealdred issued synodal canons on the eve of the conquest. The position in Normandy, as we have seen, was different. The archbishop of Rouen, Maurilius, a monk born near Rheims and with experience of Italy, had with William's backing started in 1063 a drive against the marriage of priests and other clerical sins through conciliar legislation; and Lanfranc was probably present as abbot of Caen at his two councils. It is not surprising, therefore, that legislation of this type should start in England in 1070, when the bishops were deposed, and continue for a few years after Lanfranc's appointment.

Nevertheless, it is impossible to regard this movement as the sole work of the new bishops. The first synodal decrees—and the most comprehensive—seem to have been issued at one of the legatine councils held by Bishop Ermenfrid in 1070 before the new men could have had any say. This legislation was probably inspired by William, influenced no doubt by his archbishop of Rouen and possibly by Lanfranc, and was fully to the taste of the surviving English bishops and abbots. These men had been spared because they were considered good bishops; when of foreign education they may have been impatient for some reform; and Wulfstan the Englishman was a determined reformer. In any case only the veterans knew what the common abuses were. After this beginning there was parallel legislative activity in the duchy (under Archbishop John) and the kingdom (under Lanfranc), and each influenced the other. By far the more impressive in quantity and scope was the Norman. Rouen I (1072) issued twenty-four canons, Rouen II (1074) fourteen, and Lillebonne (1080) forty-six. By this standard English legislation was meagre. Only four sets of canons, all short, are attributed to Lanfranc, and at least three of them come from the first six of his eighteen years as archbishop, from the time when English influence was still strong in the church. The record is certainly not complete. But it may be inferred that the English reformers knew that what was required in the kingdom was not so much new legislation as enforcement of the law, that more emphasis was placed on administrative action than on decrees, and that some of the canons were considered so unimportant or superfluous that they were not properly preserved. On the other hand, perhaps even influenced by the great corpus of ecclesiastical law found in England, Norman reform took a more legislative form.

The canons attributed to the English legatine council of 1070, fifteen in all, contain the main planks of the contemporary reform platform and a condemnation of a number of miscellaneous irregularities. The opening decree—that no one was to have two bishoprics—had topical interest, but was not repeated by Lanfranc; the second condemned simony; and, as though an afterthought, the penultimate enjoined clerks either to live chastely or to surrender their office. This last enactment, at least in its given summarized form, needed construing. Bishop Wulfstan, probably the most zealous of the bishops, understood it as an injunction applying to the clergy in general, and offered the alternative ruthlessly to his married village priests. But when Lanfranc turned to the problem at Winchester (1076), he reproduced the enactments of Rouen (1063), Lisieux (1064) and Rouen (1072), thus ensuring uniformity in William's lands. Village priests and deacons already married were allowed to remain so. But none was to marry or keep a mistress in future. Married canons (cathedral clergy) in minor orders were not to be deprived of their wives by force but were to be urged to dismiss them. Married canons in priest's or deacon's orders were, however, to send them away. These injunctions were a humane application of the revived discipline.

Lanfranc's decrees were largely concerned with two subjects : the life and conversation of the clergy and ecclesiastical administration. There was little legislation about monks, probably because the archbishop produced a private rule for his own convent at Canterbury, and, characteristic of the time, small concern with the laity except with regard to marriage. London (1075), cap. 6, perhaps inspired by Rouen (1072), cap. 14, prohibited marriage within seven degrees, and Winchester (1076), cap. 5, certainly following the Norman precedent, decreed that no marriage was to be performed without the blessing of a priest, otherwise the union would be considered fornicatory. Here was a clear interference with Germanic marriage custom, but with a sound moral purpose. The priest would be able to investigate the relationship between the contracting parties.

No less important than the moral and disciplinary injunctions were those dealing with administration. Bishops were to have fixed sees in cities and were to remove them from unsuitable places. They were to hold councils twice a year, appoint archdeacons and other clerical servants in their churches, and have unrestrained power in their dioceses over the clergy and laity alike. Also the procedure for compelling the laity to accept the jurisdiction of the bishop's court was declared.

Viewed as a whole Lanfranc's legislation, although fragmentary and unsystematic, does sketch the framework of a fairly comprehensive reform programme. The clergy and the monks were to observe their rules, especially chastity for the secular clergy and commonalty of possession for the monks. All forms of simony were to disappear. The authority of the bishop was emphasized at every point. There was to be orderly diocesan administration and a system of ecclesiastical courts. The bishops' synods and courts were to enforce canon law, secure the blameless clergy that was required for the ministry, and supervise the morals, especially the sexual morals, of the laity. The task was laid squarely on the shoulders of the diocesan bishop. He was given a programme and ordered to carry it out, and he was to be the master in his diocese. The novelties for the English church were not in the substance of the reforms, for English precedents can be found for most of the enactments. And, although there were certainly changes in emphasis, these were probably more characteristic of the age than of nationality. The real innovation was in ordering the creation of a new administrative machinery, purely ecclesiastical, which was to implement the reform. This policy, it must be clearly understood, reveals no hostility to the secular government. Norman custom, as controlled by William, was the model. The co-operation of the secular authorities was, quite rightly, assumed. And it was moral purpose rather than governmental ambition that dictated the choice of policy. Lanfranc's measures cannot be considered outside the context of the reform movement in the church at large, but they are almost completely independent of the narrower movement usually called 'Hildebrandine' or 'Gregorian'. They are essentially what a religious king, interpreting and modifying the views of his ecclesiastical advisers, desired to be enforced. William was one of the last reformers in the line running back through Henry III of Germany, Edgar, and Charlemagne to the Emperor Constantine.

The effects of the moral injunctions cannot be seen. Clerical marriage, still less clerical immorality, could not be destroyed by decree. But a new beginning had been made. Simony, at least in the condemned forms, was probably no problem in England, and Winchester (1076) even abandoned the subject. The immorality of the laity was Lanfranc's despair. It is the administrative reorganization of the church that is the most impressive. The Anglo-Saxon church had an old-fashioned Carolingian air. Although the distinction between Christ's law and the law of the world was clearly understood and canon law was studied as much in England as in other national churches, owing to the traditional importance of the bishops in royal government they had never thought to construct an elaborate administration of their own, but had preferred for the most part to operate through institutions which had been devised to serve royal government, both secular and ecclesiastical. William and his new bishops probably considered English custom untidy and unseemly; the king may have thought that English bishops meddled too much in secular affairs, and the prelates that in England they were denied some accustomed rights. Lanfranc, and perhaps some other bishops, brought with him to England a book of canon law less old-fashioned than those current in the kingdom. He needed its guidance for dealing with the many ecclesiastical problems which were referred to him, and for which through inexperience he was unprepared. But it should not be inferred that the new bishops had a greater interest in ecclesiastical jurisprudence than their English predecessors or were inclined to theoretical speculation. Law books were treasuries of useful texts and searched only for arguments to support a case. It was the attitude of the litigant or controversialist that determined which texts were used. In William's reign there were many litigants but no political controversialists.

The Norman church had the archbishop of Rouen at its head. In England there were two archbishops. The answer to this novelty was to get the archbishop of Canterbury recognized as primate. This scheme, which was not repugnant to Old-English practice and was eagerly pursued by William and Lanfranc, foundered on the rock of York's opposition. Documentary evidence was undoubtedly on the side of the legal equality of the two archbishops—and it needed heavy proof to upset the testimony of Bede; the papacy did not like primates (rival popes); and there was the unrelenting resistance of the church of York. So, although William cowed Archbishop Thomas, the primacy remained unstable and later seldom amounted to much. A dispute over the boundary of the two provinces was also settled in Lanfranc's favour. Had York made a real submission he might have been given a larger share of the dioceses. As it was, he was confirmed in the rule over Durham alone, and given the derisory compensation of metropolitan rights over Scottish bishops who were usually unwilling, despite papal pressure, to acknowledge their English head. More successful were reforms at the next level. The metropolitan rights of the two archbishops were reaffirmed and enforced. The archbishops took written professions of obedience from their diocesan bishops and exercised such rights over them as were allowed by current practice. Certainly by calling a series of councils, whether as primate or as metropolitan, Lanfranc showed that, under royal guidance and consent, he was the ruler of his province and of the English church.

William and Lanfranc, apart from separating Canterbury and Winchester which had been held in plurality by

Stigand, made no changes in the boundaries of the dioceses. Although pluralism was condemned in 1070, the union of Norfolk and Suffolk, Devon and Cornwall, Ramsbury and Sherborne, and the conglomeration ruled from Dorchester were all accepted. The new men did not want smaller dioceses. But the bishops, under instruction from the great ecclesiastical councils, reformed and sometimes resited their sees. The Norman bishops sat in cities, English bishops often in small places which only past history or sacred association rendered worthy of the honour. In 1072 Remigius of Dorchester moved to Lincoln and Herfast of Elmham to Thetford, in 1075 Stigand of Selsey to Chichester and Peter of Lichfield to Chester, and in 1078 Herman completed his removal to Salisbury. Little was lost and much gained by these migrations.

The bishops also appointed the cathedral officials to whom they were accustomed, including archdeacons. Although it is possible that each Old-English bishop had a chief deacon, the new bishops had a different conception of the function of their subordinates which led almost immediately to the carving up of the dioceses into territorial archdeaconries and these into rural deaneries. They appointed archdeacons and justiciars as instruments of ecclesiastical government and jurisdiction. These were the men who were to make a separate administration possible. A writ which William issued to the shires at some time between 1072 and 1076 confirmed to the bishops a monopoly of the various ordeals, gave notice that they were authorized to hold ecclesiastical cases in separate courts according to canon law, and warned the local lay officials that nevertheless they were to give as much assistance to the ecclesiastical authorities as before. The purpose of the writ was to allow the English bishops those rights which their brethren enjoyed in the duchy. These were redefined by William at Lillebonne in 1080, when he allowed the Norman bishops, besides control over the ordeals, jurisdiction over sacred places and over the offences, sins, and crimes of the clergy (except forest offences), and over the sins and matrimonial offences of the laity. No less important, he accepted that the profits of the jurisdiction went to the bishops.

Old-English bishops had possessed an ecclesiastical jurisdiction similar in scope and only different in that it had mostly and usually been exercised in the shire courts and sometimes according to secular procedures. The real change was to authorize the bishops to set up their private courts and take all the penalties instead of sharing these with the king. This reorganization was probably requested by the new bishops and willingly granted by William. He would be all the more favourable because of his desire to repress sin and crime, especially among the clergy. In Normandy he had to goad the bishops to action. In England he wanted to give them the means to act; and it may well have been considered that reform would have been hindered under the old procedures through the obstruction of lay suitors in the shire courts and even more effectively by Old-English sentiment in the hundred courts. These measures should be considered in connexion with William's other judicial experiments. He would be unaware that in this matter he was making changes that would be exceptionally difficult to modify or reverse. Throughout his rule he was either giving or taking away from the church. And just as he controlled baronial, so he was accustomed to controlling ecclesiastical justice. Even as late as 1164 King Henry II believed that he could appeal to past usage against any theory of ecclesiastical rights. No king desired to have a monopoly of jurisdiction, but all good kings considered it their duty to supervise the justice done by their vassals.

William preserved the authority of the king over the English church and also maintained intact the fruitful co-operation between the two institutions. The king and his servants were to help the church, and the bishop and his servants were to aid the king. Although the one ruled men's bodies and the other their souls, so that there was a specialization of function, both had the same ultimate ends and neither could operate in isolation or without some overlapping. Besides, the bishop was a royal vassal and a sort of baron, while the king through unction was a kind of ecclesiastical person. Some confusion was accepted as in the nature of things and aroused little comment and rarely caused strain. By and large William can hardly be said to have furthered the separation of the two orders. The new bishops had lost some of the omni-competent status which they had enjoyed in the Anglo-Saxon kingdom and, probably willingly, had been partially extricated from the comprehensive bonds of the old folk-law. On the other hand the investiture they received from the king's hands and the homage and fealty that they rendered brought them more closely than before into the ranks of the baronage. What happened later was no direct result of changes made beween 1070 and 1087. Isolated and protected as the kingdom might be, no stretch of water and no royal administrative barrier could prevent the infiltration of new ideas.

The institutions which chiefly aroused Norman censure were the monasteries. They had in varying combinations all the weaknesses most liable to provoke the scorn of monks educated in poor, austere, and spiritual houses—wealth, complacency, slackness, and an incomprehensible culture. They were often exactly the type of convent which had almost destroyed the monastic interest of Herl-win, the founder of Bec. The old and slack were judged by the young and eager and were found entirely wanting. There was no tradition in Normandy of monastic inde-pendence of the diocesan bishop, and, although many new baronial monasteries were founded while William was duke, these were certainly not outside ducal control. Moreover, with Lanfranc, an austere monk, as archbishop of Canterbury and most other new bishops somewhat un-sympathetic to monasticism the English cloisters were bound to have a rough time.

There was no set review of the abbots. William con-sidered this no business of the pope. But by 1070, through death, implication in the rebellions, and other accidents, some of the old abbots had gone, and death and the occa-sional deposition continued to thin their ranks. For some monasteries provisional arrangements lasted a long time. About 1067 William appointed Folcard, a learned monk of St Bertin's in Flanders, who had lived in England prob-ably since before the conquest, as administrator of the Fenland abbey of Thorney. But inexplicably Folcard never received blessing as abbot, was ejected about 1084, and replaced by Gunter, a monk of Marmoutier and Battle who had been archdeacon of Salisbury. The history of some other houses is equally chequered. William's original idea—probably suggested by Norman history—was to secure a comprehensive reform of English monasticism by appealing to famous houses outside Normandy to send him helpers. He colonized his own foundation, Battle abbey, from Marmoutier on the Loire, and he asked the abbot of Cluny to send him a dozen of his best men. The full significance of these moves is sometimes overlooked. It can be agreed that they are evidence for William's personal interest in monastic reform and his wisdom in searching for the most accomplished teachers. What should also be grasped is that in William's view the Norman monasteries had not the resources for the task he proposed and that the duchy as well as the kingdom had still much to learn from foreigners. We notice, too, a significant contrast in William's approach. He could provide adequate bishops from his own chapel. But abbots should have rarer qualities. This was the attitude of the pious layman.

It cannot be doubted that the refusal of St Hugh of Cluny to co-operate was a misfortune for the English church. Select Cluniac monks, free from the prejudices of the conquerors and by their background probably more sympathetic to some aspects of English monasticism than the favourite sons of new and simple Norman houses, could have reformed without inflicting unnecessary wounds. With the failure of William's more imaginative schemes English monastic reform became a piecemeal and unco-ordinated operation, in which the only policies to be seen are that William would allow no Englishman to be promoted and that the new abbots were drawn largely from the Norman monasteries of Jumièges, Fécamp, Mont St Michel, and Caen. Bec had been bled heavily to colonize Lessay and Caen in Normandy and Christ Church, Canterbury, and Rochester in England, and although it provided immediately no abbot for an English monastery its influence through Lanfranc and his circle was considerable.

As with the bishops the new abbots display the full

spectrum of merit, and, again, we can hardly believe that Lanfranc controlled William's patronage. Some of the new men, such as Lanfranc's nephew, Paul, monk of Caen, promoted to St Albans, Serlo, monk of Mont St Michel, abbot of Gloucester, and Simeon from St Ouen at Rouen, the brother of Walkelin, bishop of Winchester, first prior of Winchester and then abbot of Ely, did excellent work. A few behaved scandalously. Turold of Fécamp, appointed in succession to Malmesbury and Peterborough, left no reputation except as a soldier. And Thurstan of Caen convinced the monks of Glastonbury of the superiority of the chant of Fécamp over Gregorian plainsong by bringing in troops and killing and wounding some of the monks in their church. William sent Thurstan home in disgrace but did not have him deposed. But on the whole the men whom William appointed to the monasteries seem to have been the best available.

Monastic reform always consisted in re-emphasizing the basic disciplines in the Rule of St Benedict and modifying the customs. Both these tasks were attempted by the new abbots. They normally introduced at least some customs from their old monastery; but as the English and Norman monasteries were all of the same general family, the changes were only in detail. Lanfranc produced a set of observances for his own monastery of Christ Church which were not taken directly from Bec, but were a conflation of what he considered the best customs, and since Lanfranc was archbishop his code had a wide direct or indirect influence on English communities. But no attempt was made, as under Edgar, to achieve uniformity of observance.

These changes, and sometimes the manner in which they were made, aroused a varied amount of resentment in the English communities. The basic grievance was the contempt of the newcomers for indigenous traditions and culture. Their saints were derided, their ancient customs condemned, and their vernacular learning despised. Goscelin of St Bertin, a Flemish monk with much experience of English monasteries on the eve of the conquest, simply regarded most of the new masters as ignorant and intolerant barbarians. It has been suggested by Dom

David Knowles that the rebuilding of the monasteries by the new abbots was popular and helped to reconcile English monks to the new customs. This may have been so here and there. But some communities—and St Wulfstan is a witness to this other attitude—may greatly have resented the destruction of buildings so intimately connected with their saints and their past, and felt nothing but shame at the irreverent treatment given to their dead when the old edifices were cast down. All the same by the twelfth century most of the old foundations, when renovated by the Normans, had recovered their equilibrium and were in good heart, both spiritually and culturally. English monasticism was ready for reform in 1066; but it did not necessarily require the rough and unsympathetic treatment which it often received.

It cannot escape notice that those English houses which escaped direct Norman interference shared in the renaissance. Worcester priory under Wulfstan was at least up to ordinary Norman standards in Edward's reign and continued to prosper under the new conditions. Wulfstan admired Lanfranc and sent a favourite monk to be educated at Canterbury. There was also a rebirth of pure English monasticism which owed little to the Normans except the desire to escape from them. Some monks from Evesham and Winchcombe, neighbours of Worcester, migrated north about 1074, and they or their recruits refounded or created Jarrow, Wearmouth, Tynemouth, Whitby, St Mary's at York, and Melrose. Little immediate increase in the monastic order was due to the Normans themselves. William founded Battle on the field of Hastings to atone for the slaughter and intercede for the souls of the slain. Gundulf of Bec, bishop of Rochester, with Lanfranc's help replaced the few clerks serving his cathedral church by a monastic community. But the new barons, already attached to some Norman monastery and at first too unsettled to think of founding new monasteries on their English acquisitions, were usually content to make a donation of land to their old friends.

The internal changes in the English church were the work of William and Lanfranc and the bishops. Although the aid of the pope had to be obtained in order to remove some English bishops, even this was manipulated by William, and it is clear that thereafter no unnecessary reference was made to Rome. William had promised to see that Peter's Pence was punctually paid to the pope, and he probably honoured this promise as best he could. The archbishops had to obtain their palls from Rome. There was no more, or less, traffic between England and Rome than was usual. It was not the custom for the papacy to interfere in the domestic affairs of the national churches, unless invited or grievously provoked. William was not a man to invite or tolerate interference, and his friendly but cautious and calculating attitude towards the reformed papacy has already been discussed.

It was a time of great development within the Western church. Many projects of reform were being advocated in several circles, and although there emerged no common attitude or programme the central theme was the plight of the church and its ministers entangled in the cares and temptations of the world and subject to the lay authorities. The answers to the problem ranged from the complete renunciation of the hermit to political schemes of papal dominance over the princes. Hildebrand, who became Pope Gregory VII in 1073, although not the fanatic pictured by his opponents and perhaps louder in manifestos than resolute in action, certainly adhered to the more radical political wing of the reformers and favoured action in the world rather than abnegation. William had obtained Hildebrand's support for the invasion of 1066 in return for some promises, had flown the papal banner, in 1070 had been recrowned by the papal legates, and, together with his army, had accepted penance for the sins committed in the course of the war. These were the actions of a pretender securing and exploiting a patron. After he had made himself safe he withstood firmly and usually politely any papal act which he considered an encroachment or found inconvenient; and Gregory always gave way. This compliance is usually attributed solely to the pope's fundamental respect for William and his aims; but there was often an element of opportunist exaggeration in Gregory's actions which a resolute and reasonable man could deflate. It has been noticed that Gregory increased his pressure on William in 1079–81, after the king had suffered military reverses on the Continent. He required Lanfranc's attendance at Rome, he subjected the province of Rouen with Sens to the primacy of Lyons, and he tried to induce William to become a papal vassal for his kingdom and resume payment of Peter's Pence, which had fallen into arrears. William's answer to these overtures is worth quoting in full :

To Gregory, the most excellent shepherd of the holy church, William, by the grace of God the glorious king of the English and duke of the Normans, sends friendly greetings. Hubert, the legate you sent to me, most religious father, has urged me to do fealty to you and your successors and give better thought to the money which my predecessors used to send to the church of Rome. The latter I accept; the other I refuse. It was never my purpose, and is not now, to do fealty; I neither promised to do it, nor do I find that my predecessors ever did it to your predecessors. The money has been collected negligently during the three years I have been in France; but now that, by divine mercy, I have returned to my kingdom I am sending you through Hubert what has been collected, and the balance will be forwarded at a convenient opportunity through the envoys of our vassal, Archbishop Lanfranc. Pray for us and the state of our realm, for we have always loved your predecessors and it is our sincere desire to love you above all others and to hearken to you most obediently.

The English monk, Eadmer, writing after the close of the reign, listed some innovations for which he thought William was responsible. No one could be recognized as pope within his dominions except by his authorization. Papal letters could only be received through his hands. The primate could not issue synodal decrees in the king's absence or without his approval and sanction. No bishop was allowed to excommunicate or proceed in any ecclesiastical way against any of the king's barons and servants, even when publicly defamed of incest, adultery, or other capital crime, except by the king's command. Several other restraints on the church, such as the exclusion of papal legates except when invited by the king, the control of the movements of his bishops out of, and into, his dominions, and the prohibition of appeals from English ecclesiastical courts to the papal *curia*, were also attributed to William.

Most of these rules are abstracted from William's practice. They represent the attitude of any powerful king of the period, and, when enforced by a God-fearing ruler, were accepted without question by his bishops. It is likely that as duke of Normandy William was accustomed to more obedience from his prelates than was usual in England and that consequently he was a more effective ruler of the church than his recent Old-English predecessors. Eadmer may have been right in thinking that under William the church lost some of its freedom. But William's alleged rules only became significant later when such restraints had become less acceptable. For Lanfranc, who had learned to obey, as for most of the bishops and abbots, William was the dear lord whom it was treasonable to withstand. They had seen him act mercilessly against prelates who abused his trust; and they also knew that he had the good of the church at heart. The English chronicler recognized that William 'was gentle to the good men who loved God; . . . the country was very full of monks and they lived their life under the Rule of St Benedict; and Christianity was such in his day that each man could follow out whatever concerned his order. . . . May Almighty God show mercy to his soul and grant him forgiveness for his sins.'

Chapter Ten

The Kingdom in William's Last Years (1072–1087)

WILLIAM spent four of the first five years of his reign (1067–71) in the kingdom suppressing rebellion. After Christmas 1071 he spent less than half his time in England—probably much less than half, for although his movements between 1082 and 1085 are not well recorded it is likely that he was mostly on the Continent. He was in Normandy for three or four long periods, 1073–5, 1076–80, possibly 1082–5, and 1086 until his death; and there was no year in which he did not at least visit the duchy. After Christmas 1071 he never spent a full calendar year in England, and there were five years, possibly seven, in which he did not appear at all. There is no reason to think that William particularly liked England and the English. The conquest had caused him a lot of trouble, he had found few faithful men, he did not know the language, and clearly he did not choose to cultivate English society. It is said that he liked and admired Wulfstan, bishop of Worcester, and it is possible that there were some abbots and thegns whom he found agreeable. But, unlike Cnut, he kept himself a foreigner.

Inevitably after 1072 William seems cut down in size. He was then only forty-five years old, not much more than Edward when he started his reign, and there should have been at least a decade in which experience and acquired authority compensated for declining physical strength. But the great tide in his career had raced in and subsided. He began to appear less successful than before. To some extent this is an illusion. His early years are bathed in the rosy light of his panegyrist, William of Poitiers, and his defeats and failures have to be searched out. After the conquest his problems were more complex, and the observers of his career were certainly more critical. In England the solidarity of the campaign period began to crack and on the Continent William's natural rivals grew stronger. At the same time the native English chroniclers were commenting on his actions and they could not forbear from taking some pleasure in his discomfitures; and when, in the twelfth century, Orderic Vital rewrote William of Poitiers he introduced much spiteful and damaging matter. In truth William soldiered on much as before. The difference was that there were no spectacular triumphs to come, no striking make-weight for the occasional humiliation and the unheroic death.

There were only three really memorable events in England in the last fifteen years of the reign, the rebellion of 1075, William's arrest of Odo of Bayeux in 1082, and the Danish invasion scare of 1085–6. The Old-English annalists left 1078 blank and many years are poorly recorded. At the end of the reign they were prepared to acknowledge the good order that the king had kept; but they betray throughout a sense of oppression. There was always something to grumble about, pestilence and famine, drought and fires, heavy taxation. The Northern chronicle (*D*), written perhaps at York, came to an end in 1079. That kept at Canterbury (*E*) continued and is the only version for the period after 1079 to have survived in the original vernacular. For the exponents of the old culture the times were sad.

The rebellion of 1075 was not a serious threat to William's authority; but, as we can see from the space given to it by the chroniclers, it caused much excitement at the time; and, indeed, it can be regarded as the last phase of the conquest, for it led to the destruction of what little remained of the old political order. Because conspiracies are secret, and also because we have several accounts, the motives of the conspirators and even the course of the events are by no means clear. Least trustworthy, perhaps, is Orderic's dramatic presentation, for he attributes to the actors sentiments which are probably a generalized criticism of William's rule. The king had left England early in 1073 and his long absence was an encouragement to malcontents. The two main conspirators in 1075 were Roger of Breteuil, earl of Hereford, and Ralf, lord of Gael in Brittany and earl of Norfolk. Roger was the second son of William's old friend, William fitzOsbern, and had succeeded to his father's English estates when fitz-Osbern had been killed in Flanders in 1071. Ralf de Gael was the Anglo-Breton who had survived from Edward's reign.

Earl Roger was complaining that the king was sending his sheriffs into Herefordshire to hear judicial cases and may have thought that his earldom was not being treated with proper respect. When the trouble began, Archbishop Lanfranc, who seems to have been at the head of a regency council, ordered the sheriffs on royal authority to keep out of the earldom until Roger's complaint had been considered by the king. But this concession had no effect. The other conspirator, Earl Ralf, should have considered himself fortunate still to be in power and his specific grievances are unknown. The affair was regarded by the regents as primarily a Breton conspiracy. This may simply have been a clever political interpretation designed to spare Roger, isolate Ralf, and prepare for the ruin of other Bretons. Certainly some time after this business Count Brian, although he is not mentioned among the conspirators nor is his fate recorded, disappeared from England and his estates were given to the king's half-brother, Robert of Mortain. And the king used the rebellion as an excuse to invade Brittany in 1076. Equally obscure is the aim of the rebellion. According to Orderic there was talk of making one of the conspirators king and dividing up the land into great earldoms for the others. This is the sort of idea which could have originated with Ralf.

The plot was hatched when Ralf married Roger's sister, Emma. Although the authorities flatly disagree, it is hard not to believe that William had forbidden the marriage, at least at this particular time. The earls looked round for allies, including Denmark, and again this is likely to have been Ralf's suggestion. Among the important men at the marriage feast, bishops, abbots, and barons, was Waltheof, titular earl of Huntingdon, Northampton, and Northumberland, the other great survivor from Edward's reign. It is possible that as a man of distinguished Anglo-Danish lineage married to William's niece, and a former rebel in Northumbria, he was cast in the role of the new king. This would make sense of the plot and its sequel. But all early sources agree—although William of Malmesbury writing in 1124–5 regarded them as biased—that the earl indignantly refused to take part. He did, however, allow himself to be persuaded to take an oath not to reveal what he had heard. Technically he became guilty of concealing a conspiracy against the king. But even this crime he tried to purge as quickly as possible. He confessed the matter to Lanfranc and, on the archbishop's advice, crossed to Normandy and told his story to the king.

With the plot discovered, the two leaders raised the forces of their earldoms and the regency acted promptly to prevent them from uniting. Roger received letters of mounting urgency from Lanfranc, begging him to be a true son of his father, and was finally excommunicated. A western army under Bishop Wulfstan of Worcester, Abbot Æthelwig of Evesham, Urse d'Abitot, sheriff of Worcester, and Walter de Lassy, a local baron, kept Roger behind the Severn. While Roger was contained every effort was made to destroy Earl Ralf who had recruited troops including Breton mercenaries. The royal castles in East Anglia seem to have remained loyal and several armies were put into the field against the earl. One under William of Warenne and Richard fitzGilbert of Clare defeated some of Ralf's adherents at *Fagaduna*, presumably a perversion of Fakenham, perhaps the one in Suffolk rather than that in Norfolk; and another Anglo-Norman force, under Bishops Odo of Bayeux and Geoffrey of Coutances, pushed Ralf back from Cambridge to Norwich. The earl left his new wife in command of the castle and fled overseas, apparently to raise new troops. Norwich capitulated after a siege which may have lasted up to three months; the countess and her men were granted terms and allowed to leave the country; and the royal army, now consisting of 300 soldiers and some crossbowmen under Bishop Geoffrey, William of Warenne, and Robert Malet, lord of the honour of Eye (Suffolk), entered the castle. During the campaign Lanfranc wrote twice to the absent king:

first, that although he would dearly like to see his lord, it was quite unnecessary for William to deal personally with such conspirators and robbers since everything was under control; then, that Norwich had fallen, the war was over, and the country had been cleansed of Breton filth.

The rebellion had collapsed before Danish aid could arrive. Lanfranc sent orders to the barons to fortify their castles with men, arms, and victuals against the threat, and in the autumn the king returned. He had Earl Roger arrested and Earl Waltheof held in close custody. A Danish fleet, said to be of 200 ships under King Svein's son, Cnut, and Earl Hakon, reached York and broke into the cathedral. But this time there was no popular support and the Danes returned to Flanders. Indeed, the contrast between the English attitude in 1075 and in the period before 1072 is most marked. It is abundantly clear that in 1075 the natives in Yorkshire and East Anglia fully co-operated with the Normans in keeping order and in destroying the rebellion. They recognized that William and his men had come to stay and they now acknowledged their new lords.

At the Christmas court at Westminster William judged the rebels. The Breton prisoners were banished or mutilated. The fugitive Earl Ralf was condemned to perpetual disinheritance and Earl Roger to disinheritance and imprisonment. Waltheof protested his innocence and judgment was suspended. But on 31 May 1076, just before William left England to invade Brittany, the last English earl was taken out of Winchester and beheaded. Waltheof had spent his last months in religious exercises, his end was edifying, and in Henry I's reign a cult developed at his tomb in Crowland abbey. Waltheof's execution, although no doubt the correct fate under English law for an English traitor, is no testimonial to the quality of William's justice, so often lauded by Poitiers. It is doubtful whether Waltheof was more than technically guilty of an offence, he had tried to make the fullest amends, and the delayed sentence was barbarous by the king's own standards. We can only believe, as Orderic suggests, that Waltheof's wife, Judith, had turned against him, and that there were envious Normans who coveted his estates. As for William, the decision to execute was presumably political. He was about to go abroad again, perhaps for a long time, and he would remind all men what fate awaited those who conspired in his absence.

The fall of Odo, bishop of Bayeux, in 1082 affected the English far less but was a notable event in the king's private life. Odo quite clearly had been one of William's most trusted lieutenants in England and equally clearly had fully repaid up to 1080 his half-brother's trust. In the context both of Odo's disgrace and William's death Orderic attributes bitter sentiments and serious reservations to the king. It is in fact easy to believe that Odo became an embarrassment to William. The king was partial to entrusting government to bishops and abbots. Most of these were from time to time in command or had the direction of armies. Even the monk Lanfranc was ultimately responsible for the campaigns of 1075 and 1080, and the monk Wulfstan was with an army in the former year. Geoffrey of Mowbray, bishop of Coutances, was even more active as a soldier although his main duties were administrative and judicial. It was, indeed, impossible to take a governorship under the king without accepting some military duties. But Odo was primarily a soldier. No contemporary commentator on Odo's career considered him a completely worthless bishop. He embellished in every way his cathedral church at Bayeux. He was a patron of scholars and artists and a good administrator. In 1077, when his new cathedral was dedicated, he was probably able to display to the king and queen and their sons, Robert and Henry, the fine embroidery illustrating the conquest which he had commissioned. And it is just possible that William may have thought that Odo and his friends were a little too prominent. But, more important, William, especially when under Lanfranc's influence, was bound to have had a feeling of guilt in connexion with Odo.

William never had much difficulty in suppressing his conscience when necessity dictated. Archbishop Stigand was in high favour until his usefulness ceased. So it probably was with Odo. His loyalty and courage were indispensable during the years of war in England. But by

1082 William was probably beginning to remember that Odo had often been unrestrained, not only towards the natives in general, but also towards the possessions of the church of Canterbury, that his roughness had sometimes caused trouble, and that his mode of life, his unchastity and worldliness, was hardly to be tolerated by a Christian king. At the same time, owing to the peace, Odo's own interest in English affairs was probably diminishing. The solidarity of the royal family was breaking up. In 1077 William's heir, Robert Curthose, opened the breach which later was to grow so wide. In 1083, possibly after some quarrels over Robert between husband and wife, Queen Matilda died. William was still only fifty-five in 1082, but there are signs that he was becoming less resilient and also exasperated by his misfortunes.

According to Orderic, Odo, encouraged by Roman soothsayers, who predicted that he would succeed Gregory VII as pope, bought a palace in Rome and fitted it out luxuriously and by gifts gained adherents in the holy city. In 1082, while the king was absent in Normandy, Odo persuaded Hugh of Avranches, earl of Chester, and a number of knights to abandon their English estates and accompany him on an expedition to Rome. Although Orderic can be far-fetched in his explanation of events, this story is not so unlikely as it might appear. Opposition to the pope was widespread, especially among worldly bishops like Odo, the Normans in Apulia and Sicily were involved in papal affairs, and, whatever may have been Odo's exact purpose, we can believe that he hatched, or was drawn into, some scheme of Italian intervention. And, with all Normans aware and proud of their countrymen's achievements in the Mediterranean and Adriatic, he would have been able to recruit adventurers to go with him.

William not unnaturally disapproved. He was fairly hard-pressed by his enemies in Normandy, and Odo, whom he had left to defend England, was abandoning his post and denuding the kingdom of its armed forces. He intercepted Odo in the Isle of Wight, arrested him, and imprisoned him in the castle at Rouen. Orderic's account of the arrest is coloured by later controversies about the rights of a king over his bishops. It is, however, possible that Odo protested his immunity as a clerk and claimed that only the pope could judge him. Gregory VII in fact interceded vigorously on his behalf. And there must have been some debate about principles, for Lanfranc cited the case when William of St Calais, bishop of Durham, made a plea similar to Odo's in William Rufus' court in 1088. But William remained implacable and was reluctant even on his death-bed to grant an amnesty to his brother.

The ease with which William broke Odo is proof that there was no longer any internal threat to royal authority in the kingdom. In 1085-6, however, there was the renewed danger of a Scandinavian invasion. Svein Estrithson, king of Denmark, the unsuccessful pretender to the English throne, died in 1076. He was succeeded by five sons in turn, and the second of these, Cnut II (1080-6), had inherited his father's ambitions. He had invaded England in 1069-70 and again in 1075, and once he was king he organized a naval coalition against William including his father-in-law, Robert the Frisian, count of Flanders, and Olaf III of Norway. William may have been uneasy as early as 1082 about Cnut's intentions. In 1085 he received certain intelligence that a fleet was being assembled. He crossed to England in the autumn with an army drawn widely from France and Brittany and distributed it among the courts of his vassals. He also devastated some of the coastal areas to discourage a sympathetic rebellion and deny the invaders stores. When the fleet had not arrived by winter William dismissed part of his army; and at his Christmas court at Gloucester ordered the survey of his kingdom to be made of which an abstract has been preserved in the two volumes known as Domesday Book.

The survey was carried out in haste and with vigour. When the royal commissioners demanded detailed honorial and manorial statistics and took great pains to see that they got them, there was naturally alarm and even some ribald comment. 'There was no single virgate of land, nor indeed (it is a shame to relate but it seemed no shame to him to do) one ox nor one pig which was left out and not put in his record', wrote the English chronicler. But the inquiry hardly went lower than the men of business, the stewards, reeves, and 'farmers', men who could produce the figures; and there seems to have been no agrarian unrest. If any class was shaken it was the landlords and in 1086 they probably feared the Danish invasion even more.

William had to stay in England to prepare for the next campaigning season and his presence was probably necessary to stifle the suspicion and grumbling caused by the survey. At Easter he was at Winchester, probably the headquarters of the investigating commission; and at Whitsun he had his son, Henry, knighted at Westminster. In July Cnut was murdered in the church of Odense and the Danish threat was over. In August at Salisbury William took an oath of fealty from all the important landowners in England. When it is remembered that it was there that he had paid off his mercenaries in 1070 we may think that also in 1086 William was parading and dismissing the army and took the opportunity to increase his security before returning to the Continent. The chroniclers remembered that it was a bad year with poor weather and the plague. And, for better or worse, the kingdom was not to see William again.

Domesday Book, by omitting land north of the Rivers Ribble and Tees, shows that in 1086 the kingdom was effectively smaller than it had been under King Edward. Cumbria was outside the kingdom, and Durham and Northumbria (in the reduced sense of the term which was becoming current) were in no fit state to be surveyed. The suppression of the rebellions of 1068–71 had produced the semblance of peace in the north for about seven years. After Waltheof had succeeded Gospatric as earl and William had invaded Scotland in 1072, Malcolm of Scots kept quiet, and Waltheof and Walcher, bishop of Durham since 1071, were on good terms and co-operated well. When the earl was ruined in 1075 the bishop was appointed to succeed him. This was a heavy task even for a Lotharingian, and in 1079, while William was abroad, Malcolm ravaged down to the Tyne. Walcher's failure to meet the invasion possibly reduced his authority, and in the next year he was murdered.

We have a circumstantial account of the bishop's fate

and it illustrates well the problems of royal officials in the north. In Northumbria, owing to the strong Celtic and then Scandinavian infusions and the rough life and often pastoral economy, some primitive features of social organization, such as the solidarity of the family, the sacredness of the bond between a lord and his men, and a minute interest in the letter of the law, had persisted after they had been weakened in the more sophisticated south. The native earls traced themselves back to Waltheof I, who flourished towards the end of the tenth century, and, although the genealogical ramifications are highly complicated, they were well known. Blood feuds were common and were continued from generation to generation. It was a country accustomed to disorder, invasion, pillage, and death, yet extraordinarily resilient. Indeed, in temper the Northumbrians were probably closer to the Normans than to the southern English. But 'foreign' earls like Tostig and Walcher were held in little respect and found it difficult to avoid being caught up in the local feuds. Walcher made a bad mistake and paid the full penalty.

A thegn named Ligulf, who had lost most of his estates north of the Humber to the Norman invaders, had taken refuge on his lands in Durham. As he was related by marriage to the most distinguished nobility in Northumbria and well known for his devotion to St Cuthbert, he was welcomed by Bishop Walcher and given a post of trust in his council and in the earldom. This intrusion was resented by the bishop's existing deputies: his lieutenant in the earldom, his kinsman, Gilbert, and his ecclesiastical official, Liobwin, a Lotharingian clerk. Liobwin always opposed Ligulf in the bishop's council and court, and in 1080, after a particularly bitter dispute, asked Gilbert to avenge him. Gilbert agreed, collected his own and some episcopal troops, and slew Ligulf and almost all his household while they slept on their own estate. It is impossible to imagine in that society a more dastardly crime. When Bishop Walcher heard the news he sent messengers throughout Northumbria to announce that he was not privy to Ligulf's murder, that he had outlawed the murderer Gilbert and his companions, and that he was prepared to prove his innocence according to the ordeal proper to a bishop—presumably his personal exculpatory oath. But he did not in fact dismiss Gilbert and by harbouring him sealed his own fate.

As a result of negotiations with the kinsmen of the dead man it was agreed that both parties should meet at Gateshead on the Tyne on 14 May to hold a plea and come to a peaceful settlement. Walcher and Liobwin went with a military escort provided by Gilbert. The bishop prudently declined to plead in the open air, but retired with his clerks and his more honourable knights, that is to say with his council, into the church, and endeavoured to conduct the pleadings by messengers. The accusing kinsmen, convinced of Walcher's guilt, refused his offers, and, turning against those of his knights who were outside the church, killed all except a few who fled. The bishop then ordered Gilbert out of the church, presumably hoping to appease the mob. Gilbert obeyed and his knights followed him, prepared to cut their way through; but all were killed except two English thegns who were spared because of their race. Perhaps the church had already been set on fire, for next the bishop's clerks went out, only to meet the same end. Then Walcher ordered Liobwin to leave, and he—the one coward among them—refused. Whereupon Walcher himself went to the door of the church and asked for his own life. And when the kinsmen would not grant it, he wrapped his head in his cloak, stepped out, and fell by their swords. Liobwin alone remained in the burning church, until, half-consumed by fire, he too leaped out and died. The kinsmen were punctilious in respecting the rights of a church and avoiding some public crimes but they were determined to exercise their private right of feud and avenge the murder. Two men were reputed to have been the slayers of the bishop. The first had the name of Waltheof, but his lineage is not stated. The second was Ligulf's nephew, Ealdwulf Rus, the son of Uchtred, the son of Gospatric, the son of Earl Uchtred, the son of Earl Waltheof I. We are told that Ealdwulf was later killed by a woman (a despicable fate) and buried in the church of Jedburgh, but that Turgot, prior of Durham, had his body cast out of the holy ground. This seems to have been the end of the vendetta.

In 1080 the feud of the kinsmen of Ligulf was primarily against the murderers but also against the foreigners. From Gateshead they marched against Durham castle, built by William as he returned from the north in 1072, and tried to take it in order to kill the bishop's garrison. But on the fourth day they abandoned the siege. Norman castles were not for the taking by mobs. Nevertheless the bishop's body had to be carried by river to Jarrow for burial. When the news of the disaster reached the regency council in the south, Bishop Odo was sent with an army to punish the Northumbrians, and he carried out the usual harrying of the countryside. William returned to England in the late summer or autumn and dispatched his eldest son, Robert Curthose, to complete what Odo had begun and also to punish Malcolm of Scots for his raid in the previous year. Robert got no farther, it seems, than Berwickshire and, on his return journey, strengthened the defences by building a new castle on the Tyne.

The Normans were more than hanging on in the north. Their colonization of this wild area was thin, but they were establishing control. A new bishop, William, who had started his career in the church of Bayeux, then became a monk, rising to prior, in the monastery of St Calais, south-east of Le Mans, and finally had been abbot of St Vincent-des-prés in the same diocese, was appointed to Durham in November. William of St Calais' episcopate was hardly tranquil, but, his political misadventures apart, he brought order to his distracted diocese. He was ably assisted in the work of pacification by a new earl, Robert of Mowbray, the nephew of the bishop of Coutances.

Norman penetration of the north was hindered not only by the ferocity and relative poverty of Northumbria but also by the existence of the Anglo-Scottish kingdom of Malcolm Canmore. Malcolm, and especially his wife and sons, were ready to learn from the Norman monarchy and to follow modestly in its wake. The kingdom of Scots was a true marcher principality, for to its north and west it was fringed with Gaelic and Norse-Gaelic areas and sometimes had to look to the south for support. At the same time Norman expansion was exhausted by its conquest of Northumbria, and Malcolm and his sons were safe in that direction from all but raids and reprisals. It is clear that by 1087 nothing had been settled decisively. If Malcolm could not maintain himself against Gaelic pressure the Anglo-Norman march might be pushed sporadically northwards to take in Lothian. But if the Norman kingship weakened, the kings of Scots might easily extend their rule south into Northumbria.

Wales was an altogether different matter, and the problem was familiar to the Normans since it was like that of Norman-Breton relations. The English had already cramped the Welsh largely into the highland zone which they did not covet. And as the English borderlands were among the most fertile in the kingdom, the Welsh principalities were opposed by a thickly populated area which was attractive to the Normans. There were still some regions of Wales, notably the coastal strips, into which the Normans and English could profitably expand; but on the whole the problem was to keep the Welsh behind the boundary and prevent them raiding the richer English territory. The traditional methods in both England and Normandy were to obtain the personal subjection of the various Celtic princes, to do nothing to foster political unity, and to punish raid by counter-raid.

The Normans inherited the position created by Earls Harold and Tostig in 1063 when they destroyed Gruffydd ap Llywelyn, prince of All Wales, recovered previous losses of territory, and set up three subordinate princelings in Deheubarth (South Wales), Powys (central), and Gwynedd (North Wales). The disorder after 1066 had not substantially altered the territorial situation, and after the earldoms of Hereford, Shrewsbury, and Chester had been created to face each of the Welsh principalities, and the new honours had been heavily sub-enfeoffed, the frontier was re-established. There was, however, before William's death no spectacular advance into Wales. Most was achieved in the north, where Robert of Rhuddlan, the cousin and vassal of Earl Hugh of Avranches, had pushed on from the River Clwyd (Rhuddlan), the limit of English penetration, along the coastal strip to Degannwy, where he built a castle. Robert, aided by civil war among the Welsh, was deliberately aiming at the conquest of Gwynedd, for, as we see from Domesday Book, in 1086 he was paying the king a rent of £40 a year for North Wales. In the centre Roger, earl of Shrewsbury, pressed in a south-westerly direction and founded Montgomery, but does not seem to have crossed the upper Severn. Similarly in the south there were no great achievements. William fitzOsbern had done little before he left Hereford in 1070 to meet his death in Flanders the next year, and his second son and English heir, Roger of Breteuil, rebelled and was broken in 1075. The River Usk in Gwent, far behind the modern Anglo-Welsh boundary, seems to have been the limit of Norman advance. King William left the earldom of Hereford vacant, and in 1081 he himself invaded right across South Wales to St David's. But his purpose seems to have been essentially peaceful. He secured the release of many English prisoners and it was probably at this time that he made the treaty, recorded in Domesday Book, with the prince of Deheubarth, Rhys ap Tewdur, according to which the Welshman was to hold South Wales at a rent of £40.

Yet, although the Normans had by William's death achieved no more than Earls Harold and Tostig, the position was considerably changed. Wales and the English kingdoms and earldoms had lived together in basic harmony for centuries. There had, of course, been endemic border friction and, as in Edward's reign, occasional serious conflicts, but English Mercia had not been organized for war against Wales in the purposeful way that the Norman marcher counties and honours were. Even if the many new castles and garrisons had originally a defensive character, they were bound to serve as bases for aggression. It is possible that William, who had no wish to dissipate his military strength, did not encourage marcher warfare. Nor in the end did the Welsh principality lose its semi-independent status as a result of naked military conquest, but much more because the Welsh princes themselves became, as a result of intermarriage with the English and the cultural attraction of the English courts, little other than marcher barons and subject to the same judicial hazards. All the same the Normans were now massed against the Welsh border and after 1071 it became the only area for profitable adventure which remained in the kingdom.

From 1071 until William's death in November 1087, a period of some sixteen years, England was at peace. There was the usual disorder on the marches; doubtless there was the usual crime and violence in the countryside; but the kingdom was as quiet as it had been in Edward the Confessor's reign and for almost as long. Nor was the ordinary life of the villager or townsman much changed. The village priest and reeve and often the local 'squire' were still Englishmen, the aldermen in the boroughs were much as before. There were many English monks. Greater men than these had always been strangers, living a life of their own with their private households. That the king and the most important barons were often abroad was no concern of the agricultural or urban populations, and the changes in the episcopate did not affect the mass of the people, for they required the services of a bishop but once, for confirmation.

Yet it is likely that most men grumbled that times had changed. They could not have forgotten the harryings of 1066-71. There were the castles and their garrisons and an occasional troop of French soldiers as a reminder that it was now a Norman duke and his men who kept the peace. And there were the exactions, some harsher than before, some new. Geld was heavy. Military service was demanded perhaps more regularly and sometimes required abroad. There was the *murdrum* fine when a foreigner was found dead and the slayer could not be produced. And there was the stricter concern of the new lords with the preservation of the beasts of the chase. There was much to grumble about. But also it was said—and it was written in the English chronicle—'that any honest man could travel over the kingdom with his bosom full of gold and suffer no injury, and no one dared kill another, however much wrong he had done him. And if any man raped a woman he was forthwith castrated'. In the eleventh century crime and disorder could only be repressed by force. William's strength had been used to produce order. This was remembered as one side of the coin. But the other side also was not forgotten.

Chapter Eleven

William and Normandy

WHILE William had been conquering England his position had been worsening at home. The prospect which had been so fair in 1066, with the king of France a minor and under the tutelage of William's father-in-law, Baldwin V of Flanders, and with Anjou weak and distracted, altered entirely to William's disadvantage in the next four years. Philip I of France was growing to manhood, was jealous of the duke of Normandy, and wished to increase his hold over the border territory, the Vexin, which straddled the Seine between Paris and Rouen. Baldwin V of Flanders died in 1067, his son and successor, Baldwin VI, in 1070, and William suffered a serious reverse when the brother of the late count dispossessed their nephew. In Anjou Geoffrey the Bearded was evicted in 1068 by his brother, Fulk the Surly, a much stronger count who would not accept William's lordship over Maine. William was back in the position he had been in before 1060, on the defensive and struggling to maintain his duchy intact against the ambition of his neighbours.

William's difficulties in Normandy help to explain his behaviour in England. After 1071, even had he wished otherwise, he had little time to spare for the kingdom. He was deprived of the opportunity to study English problems and absorb the English tradition. He sometimes needed the services in Normandy of his English barons and did not allow them the time and tranquillity for settling down in the kingdom. And he required English resources, both financial and military. He was not a king like Cnut who occasionally mounted a foreign expedition from England : he remained a Norman duke who exploited his conquest for his Norman policies. The centrality of Normandy led also to much national exchange. Just as there were Bretons and Flemings enfeoffed in England, so English armies fought in Maine and the other Norman marches, and in the churches under William's sway there was considerable interchange of men. Perhaps even the English would have been included in this redistribution had they been French-speaking. Be that as it may, England remained in William's scheme something to exploit.

There is little to suggest that William had much finesse in diplomacy or could read the future better than the next man. As we have seen he greatly prized his alliance with Flanders; Flemish friendship, in view of the Viking danger, was indeed important for England's security; and William had been paying the count a money-fief of £200 a year. But in 1071 he either blundered or was out-manoeuvred. When Baldwin VI, count of Hainault and Flanders, the brother of Queen Matilda and the cousin of Philip I of France, died in 1070, his heir, Arnulf III, was young and power remained in the hands of the widow, Richildis of Egisheim. Their rule quickly became unpopular and the boy's uncle, Robert the Frisian, invaded. William sent William fitzOsbern, earl of Hereford, over to Normandy to help Matilda to cope with the problem, and when Philip raised an army to replace the fugitives, the earl joined the king with a contingent of ten knights. If Hereford thought, as Orderic suggests, that he was going to have some sport in Flanders, he was sadly mistaken, for on 20 February 1071 Robert the Frisian fell on the royal army at Bavinchove, near Cassel, drove Philip into flight, captured Richildis, and killed Arnulf and the earl. William fitzOsbern's body was taken back to Normandy for burial in the monastery he had founded at Cormeilles.

Shortly after the battle Robert the Frisian and King Philip made peace. The new count of Flanders was Matilda's brother; but William seems to have been affronted by the slaying of his steward and friend at Bavinchove and relations between the two courts remained unfriendly. Moreover, Robert, whose main interest was in his imperial fiefs and in expansion eastwards, preferred to rely for the protection of Flanders on his feudal lord, the king of France, rather than on his brother-in-law, the duke of Normandy. The alliance between the count and the French king was confirmed when Philip married Robert's step-daughter, Bertha of Holland, and the count's hostility to William was openly expressed when he gave his eldest daughter in marriage to Cnut II of Denmark, a pretender to the English crown. It was like old times when the Danish fleet which invaded England in 1075 was allowed to harbour in Flanders.

Early in 1072 William snatched his first visit to Normandy since 1067 and he may have brought Odo of Bayeux with him. He summoned all his barons from the duchy and the county of Maine to him and took their fealty, and then returned to England in order to invade Scotland. He was back again early in 1073, at last relieved from the most pressing English problems and ready to deal with Maine. Norman rule in the county was unpopular and provoked private ambitions. Important barons, such as Geoffrey of Mayenne, intrigued in their own interests and the citizens of Le Mans conspired to create a commune. Popular sentiment favoured the restoration of a native count but political necessity forced malcontents to turn in the last resort to the count of Anjou. Between 1068 and 1072 Gersent, the sister of the last count of Maine, Hugh IV, and her husband, Azzo II, marquis of Este in Venetia, tried to obtain the county for their young son. But in 1072 Geoffrey of Anjou, taking advantage of the disturbance, occupied Le Mans. Early in the following year William marched into Maine with a large English and Norman army and crushed the overt rebellion with some ease. But with Anjou and France, and sometimes Brittany, hostile, William's hold over Maine had become weak, and for the rest of his reign he was to be troubled by conspiracies and rebellions in the county, supported by Anjou.

Philip of France was prepared to do anything to harass William. In 1074 Edgar Ætheling crossed from Flanders to Scotland and was received with honour by his brother-in-law. But Malcolm was not prepared to harbour him and it was decided that the prince should accept Philip's offer of the castle of Montreuil on the border between the counties of Boulogne and Ponthieu. Edgar set off for France, but was driven by a storm back to Scotland, and this time Malcolm advised him to make his peace with William. So he travelled through England to Normandy, found a politic welcome from the king, and stayed with him until 1086, when he decided to seek his fortune in Apulia and his sister Christina took the veil at Romsey.

William returned to England before Christmas 1075 to judge the rebel earls and their followers, and came back the following spring to pursue Ralf de Gael into Brittany. With the agreement of Count Hoel V he attacked the city of Dol, where Ralf had established himself, only to incur one of his greatest humiliations. When King Philip, reinforced perhaps by Angevin and Aquitainian contingents, advanced to the relief of Dol, William retreated so quickly that he had to abandon all his equipment and suffered a loss which was estimated as £15,000. This disaster was duly noted by the English chroniclers. Earl Ralf remained the powerful lord of Gael. In 1077 William made a short-lived truce with Philip and also it seems with Fulk of Anjou.

In 1077 William was approaching his fiftieth birthday and his children were growing up. He himself was still vigorous and always hunting or on campaign. The only contemporary physical description of him is by an anonymous author, perhaps a monk of Caen, who wrote of the king's death. Unfortunately this consists of a few sentences borrowed from the last chapters of Einhard's *Life of Charles the Great*. The adapter omits all Einhard's vivid detail, introduces William's obesity, and alters just one word. Charles' voice is described as *clara* (a clear tenor), William's as *rauca* (a rough bass). This alteration must have been deliberate, but whether it was made because of knowledge or because of a view that specific voices and other humours went with certain physiques must remain uncertain. Indeed it is difficult to decide what trust, if any, can be put in this plagiarism. For what it is worth we are told (and the borrowings are in italics) that William *was just above average height with a robust and rather stout body*. Although he tended to corpulence in his later years this was not due to gluttony; *indeed he was sparing of food and especially of drink, detesting drunkenness both in himself and in others. He was ready of speech and had a good command of language. His voice was* gruff, *but less so than one might expect from his appearance.*

A generation later William of Malmesbury, again echoing Einhard, elaborates the portrait. He agrees about the king's height but is more outspoken about his obesity. William developed such a stomach that its protrusion not only harmed his dignity when standing or sitting but also contributed to his death, for some men said that during the sack of Mantes his horse stumbled and he crushed his belly on the pommel of his saddle. Malmesbury also relates that before Mantes King Philip of France jested that William was like a pregnant woman awaiting her confinement. Malmesbury agrees that the king was healthy and strong, with powerful shoulders and arms, and relates that he had a bow, possibly a crossbow, which nobody else could string, but which he could string with his feet while galloping his horse. Malmesbury adds that the king had a cruel face and was bald at the front. He also discusses current views and stories about William's sexual life and decided that the king was in fact a moral man.

If William and Matilda were indeed married in 1052, by 1077 some of the children were in their twenties, and as Robert was close to the canonical age of marriage when his betrothed, Margaret of Maine, died in 1063, he may have been twenty-four. Richard, the second son, was probably already dead, killed in a hunting accident in the New Forest near Winchester before attaining the age of knighthood (Henry was knighted at eighteen). William Rufus cannot have been very much younger than Robert and Richard. The youngest son, Henry, was in his ninth year. Some of the daughters also must have reached, or been close to, marriageable age; but the order in which the boys and girls were born has not been recorded.

William of Poitiers informs us that William took care to have his children brought up religiously. We know nothing about Robert Curthose's education, which is hardly surprising as it was a credit to no one. Robert was undoubtedly a conventional believer and his exploits on the First Crusade earned him merit. But his feckless government, under which the Norman church suffered, his foolishness and his profligacy made ecclesiastical writers ill-disposed towards him. He is described by Orderic as a short man, fat in the face and stout in body, so that he was called *Gambaron* or *Brevis-Ocrea* (Short Boot, usually rendered as 'Curthose'), a nickname said to have been given him by his father. All the same he was a bold and skilled soldier and an excellent archer. He was generous and talkative, and spoke clearly and fluently. He could also be called prodigal, shifty, and a liar.

William Rufus, although he spent some time in Archbishop Lanfranc's household, and was knighted by him, was as uncultured as his brother and aggressively anticlerical, even irreligious. Despite his basic good nature, his love for his parents, the decency of his behaviour in war, and his reputation for honour and straightness, he was a mocker at all sacred things; and this profanity together with his homosexual tastes gave him a black reputation in ecclesiastical circles. There was, it seems, an evil self-conscious flamboyance in Rufus which the conventional found deeply disturbing. He even shocked those bred in his father's thrifty household with his reckless, and sometimes senseless, expenditure. As a soldier and ruler, however, he was little inferior to his father. There was the same grit and ambition. He was another stout man, red in face, choleric, with rolling blue eyes, and a passionate, stuttering speech; undignified, a bit of a buffoon, but no fool underneath. Men learned not to underrate this young bull.

Henry, widely separated from his elder brothers by age, was certainly better educated than they. It is even possible that, as he lacked an obvious territorial inheritance, his parents may have considered putting him into the church. It does not appear, however, that Henry seriously applied himself to letters or acquired much formal learning. But clearly he developed more lively intellectual interests than his brothers and could move easily in cultivated circles. He was always aware of the teaching and aspirations of the church and was responsive to them in a somewhat administrative way. He was like his father in that the church prospered under his rule. But in his private life he was as licentious as his brothers, a cold lecher, cruel, ungenerous, calculating, in some ways the most unpleasant of them all.

It can hardly be claimed that William had much success with the religious education of his sons. He was, however, more fortunate with his daughters. The girls seem to have been both religious and also interested in letters. One of them, probably Cecilia the nun, was instructed by Arnulf who became Latin patriarch of Jerusalem in 1100. Adela especially, partly no doubt because she married into a cultured family, became a patron of writers. Baudri of Bourgueil addressed to her one of his longest poems (no. 196). The didactic tone of the 1,365 lines would, however, have deprived the poem of much appeal to the modern reader had not Baudri, when describing the countess' chamber, introduced a tapestry which recalls that embroidered for her uncle, Bishop Odo. A short poem (no. 198) to Cecilia is of less interest. If the daughters were in fact generally younger than Robert Curthose and William Rufus it seems that William as his fortunes rose took greater care over his children's education. Clearly the daughters were fitted by training to marry into distinguished families. The beauty of Adela and Cecilia, as well as their honesty and chastity, was praised by Baudri. But, as their brothers were hardly handsome, we may suspect a flatterer.

Although landed families are usually much concerned with marriage alliances, we hear little of William's plans for his children. In fact only two of them contracted a marriage before his death. The eldest daughter, Agatha (who may be the Adeliza of other lists), was affianced first to Herbert of Maine, then probably to Harold, earl of Wessex, and finally to Alfonso VI of Castile and Leon. But she died, shortly before 1074, on her way to Spain—released, according to Orderic, by the mercy of God from a fate she loathed, for Harold, whom she had seen (if true, in 1064), was the one whom she had wanted to marry. The second daughter, Cecilia, became a nun in 1075 and rose to be abbess of Holy Trinity, Caen, Matilda's foundation. The first to marry was Adela, one of the youngest, who made a suitable and useful match with Stephen-Henry, count of Blois and Chartres, in 1080, and whose third son, Stephen, was the last of the Norman kings in England, succeeding his uncle, Henry, in 1135. Rather less grand was the marriage of Constance in 1086 to Alan IV (Fergant), count of Brittany. There were no children of this union.

When William died in 1086 he had some bastard grand-children by Robert and perhaps even by Henry; but the legitimate line was then only continued on the spindle side through Adela countess of Blois. Robert married re-latively late, in 1099–1100, and his son, William Clito, was never more than a pretender to honours. William Rufus never married. Henry, who married in 1100 and again in 1121, produced only two legitimate children (of whom only a daughter survived him) to put beside his many bastards. William's apparent small concern with the marriage of his children and his failure to place his daughters more adequately needs explanation. It is hard not to believe that William was a possessive father and that he preferred to keep his children round him. He had had Robert recognized as his heir in 1066 before the invasion of England and also on a later occasion at Bonneville when dangerously ill. Robert was probably titular count of Maine as well. But William created no appanages for his sons. He believed that in his company they would learn the art of war and statecraft, and, no doubt, feared that if he gave them counties they would not only drift away and become immersed in petty busi-ness, but might also become centres of intrigue. For the same reasons he may have discouraged, even forbade, marriage. It was a convention that a man married only when he had an estate suitable for his wife's maintenance. No father was anxious to give his daughter to a landless man, and William would have been only too aware of the complications which could arise if one of his sons took a wife in his own lifetime.

William Rufus bore this tutelage loyally and no one would deny that he learned at least how to be a successful king and soldier. Robert, however, had completely lost patience by 1077. Whatever may be thought of his father's attitude, Robert became the worst kind of heir, dissatisfied, surrounded by worthless companions, always in debt, and for money prepared to serve his father's enemies. His complaints were to become the theme of so many heirs: he had not the means wherewith to reward his own men. Especially he wanted land, for his followers desired fiefs. In 1077 Robert left Normandy, perhaps after the quarrel with his brothers so vividly described by Orderic, and wandered around for four or five years with other dissatisfied men: Orderic claims that he first visited his Flemish uncles, Count Robert the Frisian and Udo, archbishop of Trèves, who died in 1078, then other kinsmen in Lotharingia, Germany, Aquitaine, and Gascony. Their gifts he wasted on parasites. William of Malmesbury adds that Robert went to Italy to seek the hand of Matilda, daughter and heiress of Boniface, marquis of Tuscany, but failed. Orderic also asserts that Queen Matilda sent her errant son remittances, apparently through the hands of one of the royal chaplains, Samson, a Breton, to whom William is alleged to have offered the see of Le Mans in 1082, and that, when the king found out, he was furious with his wife and so angry with Samson that the clerk fled to become a monk at St Évroult. If this story is true, it most likely occurred in 1082–3, just before Matilda's death. As Orderic was a monk at St Évroult and could well have heard Samson's story we can at least believe that Robert's desertion caused a great disturbance in William's household.

William had other troubles in 1077. While he was occupied with a revolt in Maine, Simon, count of Mantes, retired to a monastery and King Philip took possession of the escheated county. The River Seine as it runs from Paris to Rouen receives three tributaries from the north, the Oise, the Epte, and the Andelle. The area between the Oise and the Andelle and also to the south of the Seine was known as the Vexin. The Vikings had occupied firmly up to the Epte, thus cutting the Vexin in two. The eastern half, later known as the French Vexin, formed the county of Mantes. Some time after 1031 King Henry of France, as a reward for Norman support, had transferred to Duke Robert, William's father, the homage of Count Drogo of Mantes, and the two had been friends. Drogo died with Robert on their pilgrimage in 1035, and during William's minority King Henry had recovered the homage of Mantes. Yet the county, under its own lord, had remained a buffer in the Seine valley between the royal demesne and Normandy, and William's strategic position was much worsened when it was ruled directly by the king. It was while William was making a belated attempt to recover Mantes in 1087 that he contracted his fatal illness.

There seems also in 1077 and the following year to have been disturbances in Normandy itself, provoked by Robert. Towards the end of 1078 King Philip gave Robert the castle of Gerberoy in the Beauvaisis, north of the Vexin, so that he could annoy his father from that base. William marched after Christmas to drive Robert out, and, as Robert had collected an army of adventurers who were harrying the countryside, even Philip joined William in this task. But Robert held the allies off and in the fighting wounded his own father who also had his charger killed beneath him. William Rufus too was wounded. Englishmen were among the slain, including Toki, son of Wigod. These had been brought, presumably, by Roger, earl of Shrewsbury, Hugh of Grandmesnil, and Robert of Beaumont, who, with Robert's father, Roger, and brother, Henry, were William's leading barons on this campaign. The shock of the disaster and near tragedy persuaded these men to try to effect a reconciliation between father and son. At length William yielded and renewed to Robert the succession to the duchy. In 1080 he took him with him to England and sent him against the Scots. When William had marched through South Wales in 1081, father and son returned to Normandy to deal with Maine.

The chronology of the wars in Maine is not very clear. Orderic Vital places the following events immediately after the war of 1073 and before 1076. But he may well have been mistaken, especially as he associates them with the death of Bishop Arnold of Le Mans, who died at the end of 1081. One of William's most loyal supporters in Maine was John of La Flèche, a place midway between Le Mans and Angers and in the marches of the two counties. John had married into the comital family of Maine, and Fulk of Anjou made several attempts to capture his stronghold. Early in 1081, it seems, Fulk, with the assistance of Hoel of Brittany, took and burned La Flèche. The disaster forced William to march through Maine with an English and Norman army, including Roger, earl of Shrewsbury, and William, count of Évreux; and a pitched battle was averted only by ecclesiastical intervention. The peace of Blancheland was then made. According to report Fulk accepted Robert Curthose as count of Maine and received his homage as a lord from his vassal. It may be that William also gave hostages to Fulk as a guarantee that Angevin lordship would be respected. Those barons, including John of La Flèche, who had fought against Anjou were reconciled to Fulk, and those who had resisted the Normans to William. This peace between Anjou and Normandy, we are told, lasted for the rest of William's life : it was indeed a sensible compromise. But it was not the end of the disturbances in Maine.

In 1082 or 1083, it seems, an important baron, Hubert, lord of the castles of Beaumont-sur-Sarthe, Fresnay, and Ste Suzanne, to the north and west of Le Mans, the son-in-law of the count of Nivers, rebelled against William. Hubert, a man greatly respected by Orderic Vital, had been involved in the 1072 rebellion and had been forced by William to surrender his castles of Fresnay and Beaumont. Later he had been pardoned and appointed *vicomte*. Why he again rebelled we are not told; but he left his two northern castles, and from Ste Suzanne, much better placed to receive aid from Anjou, harassed Le Mans. William went against Hubert and when he found that Ste Suzanne was impregnable, built a town nearby to contain it. Hubert held out for three years and apparently throve on the situation. William had appointed Count Alan the Red, the Breton lord of Richmond, to command his garrison; and there were certainly some other English barons in the army, including William of Warenne and Robert d'Oilly, one of William's constables, who held wide lands in Oxfordshire and was rewarded with more for the part he played in this campaign. Hubert recruited forces from Aquitaine and Burgundy and other parts of France, and with the help of his wife's uncle, Robert of Burgundy, not only fought off all attacks but killed or captured a number of important soldiers. The ransoms of the captured provided him with an adequate income. The war, although a small affair, was clearly a drain on William's resources.

During the time of this rebellion, on 2 November 1083, Queen Matilda died and was buried in her monastery, Holy Trinity at Caen. Orderic Vital makes some appropriate and conventional remarks about her piety; but she remains a completely colourless figure. William seems to have been an adequately faithful husband and a child of the marriage was born as late as 1068. Matilda had held a position of honour and trust in Normandy since the conquest of England. But when we consider William's character and activities it is hard to believe that there was much tenderness or domesticity in the relations between the two. Her death, however, may have had one important domestic result, for about this time Robert Curthose severed completely his ties with his father.

William was in England from the summer or autumn of 1085 until the summer of 1086 seeing to the defences of the kingdom against the Danish threat. There he received first messengers from Hubert of Ste Suzanne, suing for peace, and then Hubert himself. The *vicomte* had not been defeated but was tired of rebellion, and William was glad to heal this running sore. The king returned to celebrate the marriage of his daughter, Constance, at Bayeux, to Alan Fergant, count of Brittany. And, with Maine pacified for the moment, the peace with Anjou still enduring, and with daughters now married into Blois and Chartres and Brittany, he may well have believed that he had soldiered to some purpose. It was he who had worn his enemies down. Only one problem remained, the Vexin, and an opportunity to resolve this was at hand.

The French garrison in Mantes was raiding south of the Seine across the River Eure, which was the boundary, into the diocese of Évreux, and had ravaged the lands of Roger of Ivry, William's butler and lord of Beckley (Oxon), and the town of Pacy on the fief of William of Breteuil, the Norman heir of William fitzOsbern. King William 'defied' his French overlord, claimed the whole of the Vexin, and demanded from Philip the return of the three main fortresses in the French Vexin, Chaumont, Mantes, and Pontoise. When Philip rejected the demand, William in the last week of July 1087 made a sudden attack, entered Mantes by surprise, and was then himself surprised when the Norman soldiers, always too quick with their torches, set the town on fire and put it to the sack. The church of St Mary was burned and with it one recluse. William had become unwieldy, and the heat and labour of the day brought on the illness from which he died. He was carried back to Rouen, and then, because he could not bear the noise of that busy city, was moved to the suburban church of St Gervase, a possession of the ducal abbey of Fécamp, where accommodation for him had been prepared. He was in his sixtieth year.

William suffered from a squeamishness of the stomach which denied him all nourishment. His doctors, after inspecting his urine, gave up hope. William knew that he was dying and he remained lucid until the end. He had five weeks in which to make his peace with men and with God. The earliest account of the death-bed scene has been left us by an anonymous author, probably a monk of St Stephen's, Caen, where William was buried. Orderic Vital devotes to the death and the burial one of his most impressive set pieces, in which he ranges over and judges the whole of William's life. The two writers are in rough, but not exact, agreement over William's last hours, and Orderic adds much detail, which, although probably based on sound tradition, can hardly be checked. He also provides us with an elaborate confession which certainly owes more to the writer than to the dying man.

According to the Anonymous those in attendance on the king were the archbishop of Rouen, William Bona-Anima, Gilbert Maminot, bishop of Lisieux, John de Villula, the king's doctor, later to be bishop of Bath, and the king's chancellor, Gerard, precentor of Rouen, who was to have a distinguished ecclesiastical career in England. The only layman he mentions is the king's faithful brother, Robert, count of Mortain. Orderic claims that the bishop of Lisieux and Gunter, abbot of Jumièges, were the two prelates who saw William out of the world. We also learn that Anselm, abbot of Bec, was summoned to the dying king, but, himself falling ill, never reached the hospice. That William was penitent we cannot doubt. That he admitted spending most of his life in fighting, but justified his wars, that he confessed to many sins, including the avarice implicit in conquest, but drew attention to his services to the church and offered to do penance from his wealth, is likely. According to both authorities William ordered the servants of his chamber to make an inventory of all his treasures lying, apparently, in the treasury at Rouen and in his household chamber and chapel—his money, crowns and arms, his religious utensils, service-books, and vestments. Then, it seems, in the presence of his sons, William and Henry, the king dictated his bequests to various churches and the poor. In particular William sent great gifts to the clergy of Mantes to rebuild the churches that he had burned down. He may well have advised his sons, as Orderic relates, to honour the church and always follow the counsel of good and wise men. He then divided his lands.

Here the authorities disagree in their order and emphasis, and it is safer to follow the Anonymous who had less reason than Orderic to dislike William Rufus, although, it must be remembered, he may have disliked Robert more. Rufus was present and to him the dying man gave his crown, sword, and sceptre. He also, according to Orderic, had a letter written and sealed in his presence addressed to Archbishop Lanfranc 'about appointing the king of England', gave it to Rufus, and ordered him to cross to England immediately in order to take the throne. William feared disorder in the kingdom and the machinations of Robert. The eldest son was absent, with the king's enemy, Philip of France, and it may have appeared for a time that William was going to disinherit him completely. Orderic claims that William, although sad and resentful, had no intention of attempting to deprive Robert of Normandy, to which he was the acknowledged heir. The Anonymous asserts that the king had to be persuaded by the archbishop of Rouen and the others in attendance, and agreed with reluctance. It is likely that he said some bitter words and correctly prophesied what a disaster for the duchy Robert's rule would be. Finally, according to Orderic, who was writing in the reign of Henry I, the youngest son, disappointed of land, asked what was his portion, and was told 5,000 lb of silver, a bequest, some believed, from his mother. William remained true to his policy of not creating appanages for his sons.

The remainder of the scene and the account of the funeral we owe largely to Orderic; but there is enough general confirmation in other writers to give credence to his circumstantial detail. When the king's last will had been declared William kissed and blessed Rufus and sent him on his way; and Rufus had reached the Channel port of Wissant before he was overtaken by the news of his father's death. Henry, we are told, went to the treasury in person to supervise the weighing out of his money, and busied himself with arranging a fortified treasury for its reception. So the king was left with his doctors, servants, and some barons. These asked him to release all those he held in prison, especially Morkere, the former earl of Northumbria, Roger of Breteuil, earl of Hereford, and Odo of Bayeux, earl of Kent. The king agreed to release those political prisoners who would take an oath to keep the peace in England and Normandy, with one exception, Odo. But finally, worn down by the pleading of his other half-brother, Robert, count of Mortain, William reluctantly agreed to set free Odo as well. The king took the last sacraments and sank through the night of 8–9 September; at daybreak, as he heard the bell sound for prime in the cathedral church, he died.

It is a tribute to William's authority that his power remained intact until the very end. It was with the dying man that Robert of Mortain pleaded for the release of his brother, without thought, apparently, that the new duke would probably agree to it without a care or at the worst for a bribe. But the greater the authority the greater the void when it ends. The moment that William was dead the barons left the room and hastened to their estates to protect them from the anarchy they feared. And the servants, now without supervision, stole all the furnishings of the bedchamber and, leaving the corpse half naked, fled in their turn. Orderic, not unnaturally, allowed himself some pious meditations on the vanity of human pomp and dignity. There was also panic in the city of Rouen when the news came out and a tendency to flee or at least to hide all wealth. The breakdown in authority was complete. The late king's brothers and sons were absent; his vassals and servants had dispersed. The corpse was left untended until the hour of terce. Monks from the city organized a procession to St Gervase and the archbishop ordered that the body should be taken to Caen for burial in St Stephen's, William's foundation. But there was no one to carry the order out. At last a country knight named Herlwin, for the love of God and the honour of his country, engaged at his own expense undertakers and bearers and a wagon and had the body taken to Rouen where it was put on board a ship for Caen.

Misadventure dogged William's remains. At Caen the body was met by Abbot Gilbert and a procession, but on the way to the monastery a fire broke out in the town and all but the monks rushed off to extinguish it. At the funeral the bishops and abbots of Normandy, including Odo of Bayeux, now released from prison, and Anselm of Bec, recovered from his illness, were present in force. We have no list of the laity; but it was remembered that of the sons only Henry was there. After mass Bishop Gilbert of Évreux gave the address, praising William's military achievements, his good peace and justice, and his care for the church and the weak. In conclusion he said that as no man was without sin he asked all to intercede with God for the dead man's soul and any man whom William had offended to forgive him the offence. At this a certain Ascelin fitzArthur stepped out of the crowd and complained that the land they stood on had belonged to his father and that William had unjustly robbed Arthur of it in order to found the church. Ascelin then laid claim to the land and forbade the body to be buried on his property. He was supported by neighbours. And the clergy and barons had to raise and pay him 60s. on the spot as the price of the grave and promise him as much for the rest of the land. Meanwhile the body lay on a bier waiting to be buried in the stone sarcophagus which had been sunk in the ground. When the body was placed in the tomb it would not fit owing to William's corpulence and, during the struggle to force it in, the body burst and the church was filled with a foul smell which no prodigality of incense could master. The ceremonies were completed in haste. It is not surprising that Orderic closed the eighth book of his *Historia* with some reflexions on this shabby end of a powerful man.

Epilogue

WILLIAM of Malmesbury opened his Fourth Book with the words, 'I know that many men think it foolish of me to write about the deeds of the kings of our own time and say that in contemporary history truth is often in peril and falsehood favoured, for while it is acceptable to relate the good things, it is dangerous to tell the evils of the present day.' William of Poitiers, faced with this difficulty, simply concealed or justified the Conqueror's less defensible actions. His defence, however, is interesting. Between the end of heathenism in western Europe and the beginning of the Crusades it was hard to create the image of a Christian hero out of a man stained with Christian blood. But Poitiers, whenever he could, showed William's acts of violence within the framework of a just, and even a Christian, war. With reference to the conquest of England he maintained that it was lawful, praiseworthy, and religious to destroy a perjured tyrant who was supported by a schismatic church. The Normans, because of their blend of ferocity and religious faith, and probably not through deliberate cunning or hypocrisy, were in fact in Italy, Spain, and England working towards the Crusading attitude.

This attitude, which always seems to be compounded of the highest ideals and the lowest motives, presents an almost insoluble problem to the historian. He may appear naïve if he accepts the face values and cynical if he probes beneath. To treat of a saint or a rogue is simple. To judge a man who unselfconsciously justifies his selfish actions by moral principles calls for the subtlety of the experienced confessor. William, a pot-bellied and blood-stained warrior, was also a religious man and a lover of justice by the standards of his age. Perhaps we should leave it at that. English historians face a further difficulty when writing of William, for, even after nine hundred years, all passion aroused by the Conquest is not yet spent. But the historian's prejudices have to be recognized and tolerated.

We have seen that one contemporary writer thought it convenient, perhaps appropriate, to borrow words from Einhard's *Vita Karoli Magni* and apply them to William. The two men, although hardly in the same class, are indeed from the same school; and a rhetorical passage which Viscount Bryce wrote of Charlemagne's coronation can be applied with even more justice to William's conquest of England, 'it is one of those very few events of which, taking them singly, it may be said that if they had not happened the history of the world would have been different.' If the Norman conquest had not taken place in 1066, it would never have happened at all, and the endless train of consequences for good and for evil that followed could not have been. William's expedition broke a probability of history. It was always likely that England would fall to some Scandinavian adventurer. But only in 1066 could England have been subjugated by a Norman duke. This unexpected event was at least partly of William's contriving.

Once William had died, however, it seemed that the old pattern was about to re-emerge. The duchy was separated from the kingdom. In Normandy, according to Orderic, 'the Norman barons expelled all the royal custodians from their castles and again despoiled their rich country with their own soldiers. And so the wealth that they had taken by force from the English and other peoples they deservedly lost through robbery and pillage.' Under Robert Curthose, as William had foreseen, the duchy fell into ruin.

England fared differently. Rufus was crowned king by Lanfranc and, after he had withstood a rebellion in favour of his elder brother, he established his power and maintained his father's and the Old-English traditions except in one direction : Rufus had no interest in the church, and the reform movement collapsed in England as in Normandy. Otherwise Rufus was a true son. When he had inspected the treasury at Winchester and seen the enormous wealth he had been left, he carried out his father's bequests. He gave for his father's soul ten marks of gold to each of the larger minsters and six to the smaller, and to each ordinary church sixty shillings. He also sent £100 to each shire for distribution among the poor. William's captives too were released. Rufus also gave treasure to Otto, the German goldsmith resident in England, to make a silver-gilt superstructure studded with jewels for his father's tomb, not unlike Charlemagne's as described by Einhard. The epitaph chosen to be inscribed in gold on the monument was composed by Thomas, archbishop of York. The verses are obscure as well as lame, and the description of William's sarcophagus as a little urn to hold a great king is particularly inept in view of the mishap at the funeral. We can believe Orderic when he hints that the couplets were given this honour because of the author's rank. Certainly Rufus himself could have had no other criterion.

By 1090 many of William's achievements had already disappeared. His empire was divided. Normandy was anarchical and Maine and most of the border fiefs had fallen away or were in revolt. Church reform had not only ceased in all parts but was being deliberately undone. Moreover the kingdom had again become more important than the duchy. Normandy was to pay heavily for the Conquest. Already drained of many of its best men, it was itself to be conquered time after time. Rufus and then Henry, using English resources, took it from Robert. After 1144 it was ruled by Angevin counts and in 1204 John lost it to Philip Augustus. In England the male descent from William ended with his sons and thereafter the Norman line was continued only through women.

Yet the Norman imprint on England is indelible. Roman buildings are unearthed by archaeologists, and travellers are still grateful for their roads; but Roman culture soon disappeared. The Vikings changed a few place-names, slightly enriched the English language, may have influenced the development of some institutions, improved the physical stock of the people; but we have to search for their contribution. It was the Norman Conquest which decisively changed the pattern evolving out of the fifth-century Germanic settlements, and produced that tension between two cultures—the Teutonic and Latin—which has been so creative in England.

William of Malmesbury described his fellow countrymen in these words:

> They were then (in 1066), as now (1124–5), so elegantly attired as to arouse envy, at table epicures but not to excess. They are a race accustomed to war and almost unable to live without it. They attack the enemy readily, and, if force does not succeed, destroy by tricks and bribes. At home they build large at modest cost, envy equals desire to outstrip superiors, and skin their subjects but protect them from others. They are faithful to their lords, but for a small offence quickly break faith; in misfortune they will consider treachery and for money change their mind. On the other hand they are the most kindly of all races and pay foreigners as much honour as their own; they marry into the conquered; and the rules of religion, which had died out in England, they revived by their coming. Everywhere you will see in the villages churches and in the towns monasteries going up in a new architectural style; and the country is so flourishing under the new customs that any nobleman would consider the day lost which he did not glorify with some splendid achievement.

The Normans had indeed the prime qualities of a master-race: the confidence of natural rulers and the adaptability which springs from confidence. William was, except for a Breton strain, of almost pure Scandinavian descent. But the descendants of Rolf had travelled far. The most acquisitive of races, they had taken from their neighbours, and even from distant peoples with whom they had made contact, every idea that seemed useful to them. Pragmatic and utilitarian, they dropped any custom which did not work. So their stock of ideas was always that best suited to the conditions in which they found themselves. It was never an armoury distinguished by refinement or sophistication. Soldiers ask for sturdy weapons, simple plans, uncomplicated organization. And it says much for Norman direction that clever churchmen, brilliant artists and architects, all the foreign technicians they recruited, learned to serve their patrons in the direct idiom that was required.

With these qualities the Normans could not fail to leave their mark on England. They were prepared to learn and also to teach, indeed teach sharp lessons. Like most creative conquerors they were ready to build. The mottes of Norman castles have not yet been eroded. The Tower of London still stands. No architectural style is easier to recognize in churches than Norman romanesque. Its simple geometry enlivened by barbaric ornament, its stoutness and rough execution, the unexpected height of some chancel arches, impress and satisfy. It is uncomplicated, yet assured and sometimes daring.

Although the Normans came late into a settled countryside, they still managed to leave their trace. Anglo-Saxon village names often remain compounded with the names of Norman owners. In the social sphere Norman influence is inevitably less tangible. But there are today Englishmen who are proud to claim ancestors 'who came over with the Conqueror'; French is the common second language in England; and children are christened William, Robert, and Henry more often than Edgar, Edward, and Harold. The Norman aristocracy for long set a pattern to be imitated by their inferiors. Hence the English language itself owes almost as much to French as to Old-English and has a larger vocabulary than any other.

The Normans, because they carried some potent traditions, enriched most spheres of English life. Few countries had a more eclectic civilization than medieval England. No region has been so delicately poised, and for so long, between the pull of the Germanic north and the Latin south. Basically, despite the Normans and their French successors, England has remained Teutonic in social attitude and religious feeling. The people sense their kinship with the northern races of Europe. But they have almost always looked to the south for artistic inspiration, attracted by the passion, frivolity, logic and clarity, the colour of the Latin scene. William the Conqueror had little of this Latin panache. Lanfranc learned to subdue it. But William, by widening the roads to the south and bridging the Channel, opened England to influences which were to carry her into a new age, the age of French civilization.

Select Bibliography

A. *Bibliographies*

The Norman Conquest has attracted much attention and aroused many controversies. The following bibliography is short and arbitrary because the student wishing to pursue any particular branch of the subject must use lists far more comprehensive than can be provided here. He will find of greatest use W. Bonser, *An Anglo-Saxon and Celtic Bibliography (450–1087)* (1957) and David C. Douglas, *William the Conqueror* (1964), pp. 3–7, 427–47. There are valuable bibliographical essays on aspects of Norman history in *Bulletin de la Société de Normandie*, xxxvi and xxxvii (Caen 1926, 1929). Reference should also be made to *English Historical Documents*, ii (1953), ed. Douglas and G. W. Greenaway.

B. *Primary Sources*

The basic contemporary narrative accounts are William of Poitiers, *Gesta Guillelmi*, edited and translated into French by Raymonde Foreville (Les classiques de l'histoire de France au moyen age, Paris 1952), William of Jumièges, *Gesta Normannorum ducum*, ed. Jean Marx (Rouen and Paris 1914), and *The Anglo-Saxon Chronicle*, ed. Dorothy Whitelock, etc. (1961), with a Latin version in Florence of Worcester, *Chronicon ex Chronicis*, ed. B. Thorpe (Eng. Hist. Soc. 1848–9). Two important historians of the next generation are Ordericus Vitalis, *Historia Ecclesiastica libri tredecim*, ed. A. Le Prévost (Collection de la société de l'histoire de France, Paris 1838–55), particularly valuable because it preserves some of the lost final pages of William of Poitiers, and William of Malmesbury, *De Gestis regum Anglorum*, ed. W. Stubbs (Rolls Series, 1887–9). The fundamental documentary evidence is presented, for Normandy, in *Recueil des Actes des Ducs de Normandie de 911 à 1066*, ed. M. Fauroux (Société des Antiquaires de Normandie, 1961) and, for England, in *Regesta Regum Anglo-Normannorum*, ed. H. W. C. Davis (1913). The pictorial evidence of *The Bayeux Tapestry*, ed. Sir Frank Stenton (1957), should not be neglected. The value of some of these sources is discussed by Sten Körner, *The Battle of Hasting, England, and Europe, 1035–1066* (Lund 1964).

C. *Biographies*

E. A. Freeman's *The History of the Norman Conquest* (5 vols., 1867–79) contains the most voluminous treatment of the Conqueror, but is almost unreadable today and is also treacherous except for the expert. More recent works are Sir Frank Stenton, *William the Conqueror and the Rule of the Normans* (1908) and David C. Douglas, *William the Conqueror* (1964).

D. *General Histories*

In order of date, W. J. Corbett, 'The development of the duchy of Normandy and the Norman Conquest of England', *The Cambridge Medieval History*, V (1929), ch. XV, Sir Frank Stenton, *Anglo-Saxon England* (1943), Frank Barlow, *The Feudal Kingdom of England 1042–1216* (1961), and H. R. Loyn, *Anglo-Saxon England and the Norman Conquest* (1962), are useful for the wider setting.

E. *Specialist Studies*

Only a few of the most important or recent works can be listed. C. H. Haskins, *The Normans in European History* (New York 1915), and *Norman Institutions* (Harvard 1918) are still valuable. For Normandy's neighbours, see F. L. Ganshof, *La Flandre sous les premiers comtes* (Brussels 1943), J. Dhont, 'Les Relations entre la France et la Normandie sous Henri I', *Normannia*, xii (Caen 1939), A. Fliche, *Le Règne de Philippe I* (Paris 1912), J. Boussard, 'La Seigneurie de Bellême aux Xe et XIe siècles', *Mélanges d'histoire ... dédiés à L. Halphe*n (Paris 1951), R. Latouche, *Histoire du comté du Maine pendant le Xe et le XIe siècle* (Paris 1910), L. Halphen, *Le comté d'Anjou au XIe siècle* (Paris 1906), and A. de la Borderie, *Histoire de Bretagne* (Rennes 1896–1914). For a study of feudalism, see M. Bloch, *La Société féodale* (Paris 1939–40). In the field of constitutional history, H. G. Richardson and G. O. Sayles, *The Governance of Medieval England* (1963), are iconoclastic and amusing. R. Lennard, *Rural England, 1086–1135* (1959), surveys the economic scene. V. H. Galbraith, *The Making of Domesday Book* (1961), sums up his studies of the mechanics of that record; R. Welldon Finn, *The Domesday Inquest and the Making of Domesday Book* (1961), deals more with its contents. On the ecclesiastical side reference may be made to H. Böhmer, *Kirche und Staat in England und in der Normandie im XI. und*

XII. Jahrhundert (Leipzig 1899), David Knowles, *The Monastic Order in England* (1940), Z. N. Brooke, *The English Church and the Papacy from the Conquest to the Reign of John* (1931), A. J. Macdonald, *Lanfranc* (1944), and R. W. Southern, 'Lanfranc of Bec and Berengar of Tours'. *Studies in Medieval History presented to F. M. Powicke* (1948). For more extensive lists consult the bibliographies mentioned in section A above.

Index

Persons are indexed under their Christian name.
Abbreviations: abp = archbishop, abt = abbot, bp = bishop,
ct = count, ctess = countess, d. = duke, k. = king

ENGLAND AND NORMANDY

Miles
20 0 20 40 60 80 100

Kilometres
20 0 20 40 80 120 160

Melrose

Jedburgh

Hexham Newcastle
Tynemouth
Gateshead Durham
R. Tees Whitby

Richmond

R. Ouse York Stamford Bridge
Fulford
Pontefract

R. Ribble Chester

Rhuddlan

R. Dee

Montgomery Shrewsbury
R. Severn

St Davids Hereford Worcester
Gloucester
R. Usk
Bristol Wells

Glastonbury Malmesbury

Montacute Salisbury

Exeter Sherborne

Lincoln

Nottingham
Lichfield Crowland
Warwick
Evesham Northampton
Winchcomb Huntingdon
Clare

Ramsey

Elmham

Thorney Norwich
Peterborough
Thetford
Ely
Cambridge

Berkhamsted
St Albans
Rochester London
Wallingford Westminster

Dorchester Canterbury
Winchester Dover
Chichester Romney

Battle
Wissant

FLANDERS Ghent
Bruges